Praise

The Essence of Courage

Reading Lynn Watson's devotions is almost like a spa day. Her expertise and unique approach bring relaxation and renewal to the spirit and the body.

~~Johnnie Alexander, Award-winning author, *Where Treasure Hides, Where She Belongs, When Love Arrives*

I LOVE this book. I'm stunned at Lynn's creativity and knowledge. It is one of the most unique books I've had the privilege to read. It's so fresh, interesting, captivating, and inspired.

~~Jeanne Newberry, Pastor's Wife, Bellevue Arlington, Satellite church of Bellevue Baptist Church, Memphis, Tennessee

I am on Thanksgiving break this week, and I am visiting my in-laws in Kentucky on their 150 acres of land. It is so beautiful here, and I have treasured my quiet time with my coffee, reading the book and enjoying the beautiful sites around me. I loved the Essence Droplets. Lynn shared a lot of fun activities and great information. During that part of the book, I felt like I was reading an Experimental Devotional. Lynn is an incredibly gifted writer. I'm so grateful that she chose me as one of her early readers.

~~Jennifer Cavitt, Bartlett, Tennessee

I really like the book. It is very different, easy to read and it does draw me in. Also, the cover, I love. I would definitely recommend it and give it as a gift.

~~Sammy Gordy, Women's Ministry Assistant, First West Church, West Monroe, Louisiana

I've only begun to read this morning and I'm already all in!!! Lynn!!! Thank you for saying 'Yes!' to this God moment idea given you.

~~Sharron Baker, Bartlett, Tennessee

This book is definitely for those of us who desire to go to a deeper level in our walk with Christ. How the author intertwines the "essence" of oils with the fruit of the Spirit, and connects Galatians 5 with Proverbs 31 is incredibly amazing! I can't wait to sit down with Jesus and a group of women and dig into our "locked gardens!"

~~Joyce Letcher, Bible study leader, retired nurse, Boise, Idaho

LOVE THIS DEVOTIONAL!!! this is the FIRST time my daughter actually wants to do a study with me, and I cannot say thank you enough for that.

~~Noelle Norton, Home School Mom

There are your Bible studies, lectures, groups, homework... And then there is The Essence of Courage...! Kitchen tables and coffee and wonderful scents wafting thru the warmth of all your best friends talking and sharing their hearts. Everyone comes away with the courage that comes from experiencing the depths of God's love in His word and in all our lives.

~~Robin Mokry, die-hard avoider of women's groups, Boise, Idaho

Inspirational Collection for Women: Volume 1

The Essence of Courage

Cultivating the Fruit of the Spirit in Solomon's Locked Garden and in Your Heart

Lynn U. Watson

Front Cover Illustration by Allisha Mokry

Dedication

Many called her their best friend.
Every tribute praised the overflowing evidence of
Holy Spirit fruit in her life.
She went to be with Jesus during the writing of this book.

Dedicated to the memory of my dear friend,
Jorgette Brooks
1956-2016

Contents

Introduction

Thank you for taking the time to read the introduction.
You'll be really glad you did, because it contains
important information for my inspirational
collection to make sense.

--*Cinnamah-Brosia*

Essence and Courage Defined

Essence – noun – **es** ens

1. The basic real, and invariable nature of a thing or its significant individual features
2. A substance obtained from a plant, drug or the like by distillation, infusion, etc. and containing its characteristic properties in concentrated form.
3. Solution of an essential oil
4. A perfume scent
5. The inward nature, true substance, or constitution of anything as opposed to what is accidental, phenomenal, illusional, etc.
6. Something that exists, especially a spiritual or immaterial entity

Courage – noun – **kur**-ij

1. The quality of mind or spirit that enables a person to face difficulty, danger, pain, etc., without fear; bravery
2. The heart as the source of emotion
3. Have the courage of one's convictions, to act in accordance with one's beliefs especially in spite of criticism

King Solomon spoke of his bride as a locked garden full of essence of courage. Wonder which essences of courage are locked in your garden? Join us at Cinnamah-Brosia's coffee cottage and find out!

Dear Reader,

I'm so excited you're here, and so thankful for each and every one of you. I've been praying for you for a long, long time.

God wove the story of essential oils into our world on the third day when He created vegetation on the earth. Twelve years ago essential oils intersected a crossroads in my life. Growing knowledge of them opened Scriptures in a meaningful, new way. I found myself particularly fascinated with the locked garden filled with its fruits, spices, and essential oils described in Song of Solomon. These dozen trips around the sun, God nudged me to share a fresh perspective. The vision evolved into something quite different from the original plan. I'm certain it is exactly as God intended. By a series of "God-incidences," He released this work in His perfect timing and by His inspired design.

Consulting several Bible commentaries confirmed my light bulb moment. The gifts from Solomon's garden represent the fruit of the Holy Spirit.

The characteristics of each spice, oil, and fruit connect them to the Galatians 5 list in exactly the same order. Solomon's mom, Bathsheba, advised her son what to look for in a Godly wife. Her list of virtues (Proverbs 31:10-31) closely paralleled Solomon's description of his bride and the produce shopping list of Galatians.

But the fruit of the Spirit is love, joy, peace, patience, kindness,
goodness, faithfulness, gentleness, self-control;
against such things there is no law.
(Galatians 5:22, NASB)

My sister, my bride, you are a locked garden — a locked garden and a sealed spring. Your branches are a paradise of pomegranates with choicest fruits, henna with nard—nard and saffron, calamus and cinnamon, with all the trees of frankincense, myrrh and aloes, with all the best spices. You are a garden spring, a well of flowing water streaming from Lebanon.

(Song of Solomon 4:12-15)

Did Solomon remember his mother's words, while he poetically spoke about fruits, spices and oils? Mom's words reflected practicality. When heeded, they would protect his integrity, earn him respect, prosper him, and produce a Godly home with children who, prayerfully, also loved and served The Lord.

His mother, Bathsheba, was from a Jewish family. Her husband, father, and grandfather played key roles on King David's team. As a result of an impulsive and adulterous action, she was violated, impregnated, widowed, remarried, and had mourned the death of her first son before she bore Solomon.

This married woman was bathing nude on the roof of her home across from the king's palace. Her alluring action may have been unintentional, but attracted King David's attention. The temptation was too great for both of them and resulted in an unplanned pregnancy. His plot to cover up "the problem" failed, and the king issued orders for her husband's murder. For King David, "the man after God's own heart," this was the biggest recorded mar against his name. More importantly, it was a sin against God! To King David's credit, he did marry her. Their young son lived only a short time. Hopefully, she shared in the king's sincere repentance and God's restoration. You'll find them recorded in Psalm 51 and Psalm 32. Their story is written in 2 Samuel 11-12.

After their mourning period, Bathsheba conceived again. They named the child Solomon – a derivative of Shalom – the Hebrew word for peace. The reason God allowed polygamy in the Old Testament is unknown. King David had many wives and many children; but he promised Bathsheba, Solomon would be his successor to the throne.

Having learned from the mistakes of her own life, she guided and encouraged her son in wisdom and Godliness. Her pre-marriage counseling has become known as the Proverbs 31 Woman.* Bathsheba was further honored by her inclusion in the genealogy of Jesus.

Connecting the dots between his mom's sage wisdom, the special treasures of Solomon's locked garden, and his bride enriches our perspective. The woman described in Proverbs 31 is the absolute ideal woman. Yet, like you and me, her humanity would have kept the real woman from attaining those lofty goals every time. Like Bathsheba and like us, she would have failed, asked forgiveness, and found restored relationship with God many times.

As a role model for us – no matter our generation, marital status, family, vocation, or profession – we've created Cinnamah-Brosia. Real women provided her stories. She represents the Godly woman madly in love with Jesus. Her life wafts out the essence of courage of the fruit of the Holy Spirit in her life. She shares wisdom learned from her own mistakes, repentance, and restored relationship with Jesus. She's the proprietor of a wonderful little coffee cottage and gift shop, tucked into an openly inviting garden in the heart of her community. She's always eager to make new friends and prays you'll find the friendly and casual atmosphere an inviting place to hang out.

For each fruit, spice, and oil Solomon mentions, we've provided four different looks into its connection to the fruit of the Spirit, women of the Bible, and application to our own lives. Within that context, Cinnamah-Brosia shares stories from her life and that of her friends and family. We pray you will find the essence of courage for the challenges of your own life.

Blessings,
Lynn

The Proverbs 31 Woman
(Proverbs 31:10-31*, NIV)

A wife of noble character who can find? She is worth far more than rubies. Her husband has full confidence in her and lacks nothing of value. She brings him good, not harm, all the days of her life. She selects wool and flax and works with eager hands. She is like the merchant ships, bringing her food from afar. She gets up while it is still night; she provides food for her family and portions for her female servants. She considers a field and buys it; out of her earnings she plants a vineyard. She sets about her work vigorously; her arms are strong for her tasks. She sees that her trading is profitable, and her lamp does not go out at night. In her hand she holds the distaff and grasps the spindle with her fingers. She opens her arms to the poor and extends her hands to the needy. When it snows, she has no fear for her household; for all of them are clothed in scarlet. She makes coverings for her bed; she is clothed in fine linen and purple. Her husband is respected at the city gate, where he takes his seat among the elders of the land. She makes linen garments and sells them, and supplies the merchants with sashes. She is clothed with strength and dignity; she can laugh at the days to come. She speaks with wisdom, and faithful instruction is on her tongue. She watches over the affairs of her household and does not eat the bread of idleness. Her children arise and call her blessed; her husband also, and he praises her: "Many women do noble things, but you surpass them all." Charm is deceptive, and beauty is fleeting; but a woman who fears the Lord is to be praised. Honor her for all that her hands have done, and let her works bring her praise at the city gate.

Most Bible versions present this section of Scripture as written to Lemuel by his mother. It is believed that Lemuel was a nickname Bathsheba had for her beloved child.

Meet Cinnamah-Brosia

The idea that Solomon's bride and the woman described by his mom in Proverbs 31 each portrayed the image of a super hero bride caught my attention as I began bringing this book to life. By all appearances, they perfectly embodied all the fruit of the Spirit. Solomon's description and his mom's checklist (Proverbs 31) depicted "Miss Personality" with an impossible-to-measure-up character. My next step was to create a fictional character resembling her. Unfortunately, no one would choose to befriend "Miss Perfect." No blame placed there.

Instead, Cinnamah-Brosia emerged. Created from many women's stories, her character is authentic. She lives, works, and plays in the real world, and would love to call you her friend. Her real name (but no one uses it) is Cinnamon Amber (Porter) Fields. Summers at Gram and Gramps highlighted her tough childhood and helped define who she has become.

Our friend is well-liked and appears near perfect to some. In reality, she represents you, me, the Proverbs 31 woman, and Solomon's bride. She's a real flesh and blood woman who recognizes her shortcomings and fears. She's a daughter, sister, granddaughter, wife, mother, former nurse, coffee shop owner, and wears plenty more hats too. She experiences life's challenges, sometimes handling them better than others, but she learns from them. She knows great sorrows and celebrates great joys. She needs the same Godly courage we do.

While all three of the Scripture sections mentioned paint beautiful word pictures suitable for framing, we can be sure Solomon's bride harbored her own imperfections, doubts, and fears. His mom and her version of her son's "model wife" faced them too. Not one of us displays every single fruit of the Spirit all the time, either.

Admiring the lovely verbiage of these Scriptures, without embracing their truths, we avoid our fears – fear of not measuring up, fear of rejection, fear of failure, fear of disappointing, fear of disappointment, fear of the what ifs, fear of _____(you fill in the blank).

Just like Solomon's bride and his mom would have done before her, Cinnamah-Brosia gathers wisdom from the lessons and circumstances life tosses her way. She allows the work of the Holy Spirit to bloom in her heart. Cultivation of Holy Spirit fruit produces the essence of courage we all need to live victoriously in spite of what's happening at the moment.

As we meet her on the pages of this book, Cinnamah-Brosia had been helping her Gram, Miss Dot, run her café, which opened in the 1960s. Inspired by her Gram's sweet memories, "C-B" renovated the café after Gram's passing and reopened as Cinnamah-Brosia's Coffee Cottage and Gift Shop.

Frank, the always-humming editor of the local paper, made sure to attend the grand reopening. A few mornings later, Jane, her trusted right arm at the cottage, came in waving a copy of the *Pearlville Weekly*. "So, this is what it's all about? I love the story of your name." Jane leads a small group Bible study at the café on Tuesday evenings and had to ask, "Do any of the ladies in our small group even know?"

Reno Complete: Cinnamah-Brosia's
Coffee Cottage & Gift Shop Open

Cinnamah-Brosia's Coffee Cottage and Gift Shop hosted a well-attended grand reopening on Saturday, October 1. The coffee cottage is the former Miss Dot's Café. Gram and "C-B's" daughter, Kaitlyn, planned the redo prior to Miss Dot's passing. The walls have been refreshed in frothy cappuccino. Regulars will remember Sophia's Corner, a favorite gathering spot at the café. With a coat of white paint, the stone fireplace is still the cottage's focal point and even more inviting. The comfort of the gingerbread leather sofa and two overstuffed turquoise chairs filled with berry-trimmed vanilla accent pillows beckon you in. Kaitlyn's creativity has turned the old round wooden coffee table into a work of art. The pomegranate border was inspired by Gram's ambrosia recipe.

The addition of a gift shop provides convenience to customers. Currently, you will find garden items, artwork, books, jewelry, and kitchen gadgets. Kaitlyn is managing the gift shop and promises to keep the inventory fresh and exciting.

Cinnamah-Brosia's name is really Cinnamon. Her Gram, Miss Dot, prayed the name as a blessing over the child when she was three years old. The suffix "ah" in Hebrew means "of God." Cinnamon representing goodness, Miss Dot reinvented the name and trusted she would witness a harvest of the goodness of God in her granddaughter's life.

Everyone who visited Miss Dot's Café remembers her ambrosia. Cinnamah-Brosia recalled, "I requested her 'brosia every day during my childhood summer visits. Ambrosia is full of fruit reminding my Gram of the fruit of the Spirit. The name is a mouthful, I know, but she put the two words together. Others found ways to shorten it, but to Gram and Gramps I was always Cinnamah-Brosia. I really do love all that it meant to them."

With the transformation come many opportunities for the people in the community to meet and hang out. The menu of scrumptious baked goods and both hot and chilled beverages guarantees a line forming every morning. The pleasant vintage space will be available for community events in the evenings. Cinnamah-Brosia's Coffee Cottage will serve guests from 6:30 AM to 2 PM each day.

It's easy to imagine Miss Dot proudly smiling down on her granddaughter today.

Beginning on page 176 you will find a full profile of Cinnamah-Brosia. It's a great reference as you read through her stories.

Hints for Using this Inspirational Volume

Following an introduction to Solomon's mom, Bathsheba, each fruit, spice or oil from the garden and its corresponding fruit of the Spirit is presented in four parts.

1. Cinnamah-Brosia and Friends Share Their Stories: She and her friends introduce us to a fruit of the Spirit and share their own stories about that fruit in their lives. *(All the stories in the "Cinnamah-Brosia and Friends Share Their Stories" sections are based on events shared by real flesh and blood women. The stories have been fictionalized to fit our characters and timelines appropriately and to protect actual identities.)* They prepare us to discover the essence in Scripture and to meet a woman of the Bible who also displays the representative fruit of the Spirit. "C-B" loves essential oils, baking, music, and God's Word. She spreads that love around. In these sections you will become better acquainted with her, learn what she's diffusing, and discover the café's special of the day, a song that's playing, and the Scripture verse she's posted. *(The oils chosen for diffusing may not be the same one featured for that fruit, but they are ones typically readily available and complement the fruit of the Spirit for that selection. Songs playing are an eclectic variety of old and new. We hope you will recognize some, and others will become new favorites. Just like "what's diffusing," each song was chosen to complement the fruit of the Spirit for that selection.)*

2. The Essence in Scripture: a devotion that speaks of the fruit, spice or oil in context of Scripture. All personal stories included in "The Essence in Scripture" sections are drawn from the author's own experiences, and are true.

3. A Woman of the Bible Displays the Fruit: a devotion featuring a woman of the Bible whose story exemplifies that particular fruit of the Spirit. All personal stories included in "A Woman of the Bible Displays the Fruit" sections are drawn from the author's own experiences, and are true.

4. Essence Droplets: a collection of fun facts about each fruit, oil or spice; and "Your Turn" – practical ways for you to incorporate them into your world.

Residing between the lines of the Bible stories are real people like you and me. Consideration was made regarding how their lives may have been impacted by their culture and how they may have interacted with each other. Certainly, details may have been different than depicted, but the ones shared are definitely plausible.

A friend commented, "You have chosen different women than I would have to represent each fruit, but they connect perfectly. There's something to learn from each one. Each fruit is needed at different times and in different circumstances. In these snapshots, we see each woman of the Bible in a different light than the picture we may have in mind. We see each other in different lights, too. Thank you, Heavenly Father, You see us through the Light of Jesus."

Chapter 1

Pomegranate - Love

Cinnamah-Brosia and Friends
Share about Love

Diffusing Today: Juniper and Orange

Aromatic Influence: The aromas of evergreen and citrus may help fill the room with a sense of joy, peace, and harmony

Daily Delight: Orange Pomegranate Scones

Musically: Jesus Loves the Little Children ("Veggie Tales: 25 Favorite Sunday School Songs!")

Verse of the Day:
> *Dear friends, let us love one another, for love comes from God.*
> *Everyone who loves has been born of God and knows God.*
> (1 John 4:7, NIV)

She contemplatively picked at her cinnamon roll and barely sipped her peppermint hot chocolate. I adored the usually quite precocious and happy child. Today, fear spilled out of her questions. The conversation with her mom went a little like this. Almost in tears, Lily questioned: "But what if she doesn't like me? I don't even know her." A photo of another little girl filled the screen of Mandy's phone.

"Beautiful little girls – both of them."

Mandy invited me to "meet" Vanessa. "Vanessa's family serves as missionaries in Brazil. Lily has seen pictures of the jungle conditions there. Our pastor has a connection to the family, and with his encouragement, our church is supporting them. Chase and I readily agreed to be our church connection for this family, keeping in touch to encourage them and pray for their needs. How perfect for Lily and Vanessa to be friends, too, don't you think?"

"Lily, does that idea scare you? I heard your question to your mom."

"Oh, it does, Ms. CinnaBro. What would I say, and what if she doesn't like cinnamon rolls? Look at her home. I bet she doesn't have a hula-hoop or a pretty doll, and doesn't go to birthday parties. If I tell her about my life, she might not like me very much at all."

"Mr. Jeremy and I felt the same way a few years ago when we chose to provide a link between our church and missionaries we didn't know. We wondered how in the world we got into this whole thing. It seemed simple enough when we said 'yes,' but then we really had to meet them on the computer or in a letter or something. We wondered what they would think about us. Their life was very different from ours. Not sure why, but that was scary. So, what do you think we did first, Lily?"

"Did you cry to your stuffed animals?"

"Well, no. I have reacted like that sometimes, but instead, we prayed for them – every morning. Know what surprised us the most? Within three weeks, we loved this family just like Jesus knew we would. He answered our prayers, by answering a prayer we didn't even know to pray. 'Jesus, help us love these people.' Now we can't wait to chat online. We love the opportunities to send special goodies to them when someone is traveling that way. Do you think you could pray for Vanessa?"

"Sure, I can do that. Do you believe she will love me, too?"

"That's exactly what I believe, Lily. BFF's!"

God knows how much I love you and long for you with the tender
compassion of Christ Jesus.
(Philippians 1:8, NLT)

The Essence of Pomegranate in Scripture
Ruby Red Seeds of Love

Botanical Name: punica granatum;
native to Persia and Western Himalayans

God is love, and God loves ruby red pomegranates! If I were the designer I would incorporate what I love. First mentioned in Exodus, pomegranates were included in God's design for the priest's robe. Embroidered around the hem in blue, purple, and scarlet, pomegranates were displayed among the gold, jewels, and engraved pieces vital and significant to the priestly garments.

> *"Make pomegranates of blue, purple, and scarlet yarn on its lower hem and all around it. Put gold bells between them all the way around, so that gold bells and pomegranates alternate around the lower hem of the robe. The robe must be worn by Aaron whenever he ministers, and its sound will be heard when he enters the sanctuary before the Lord and when he exits, so that he does not die."*
> (Exodus 28:33-35)

Listen closely...do you hear the gentle tinkling of the gold bells between the pomegranates? Incredible love and utmost respect accompanied him as the priest entered the Holy of Holies. The presence of the God who loved all mankind resided in that exact place. The sight and sound pleased and glorified the Father.

The history of pomegranates dates back to 3500 BCE, making them one of the first cultivated fruits. Attached to that history is a treasury of fact and lore. Pomegranates appeared on Jewish coins,

Solomon fashioned his crown like one, and 200 of them were carved on each colonnade of his temple. In mythology they represented permanency of love. Each fruit contains many seeds – some legends say 613 – significant of the number of commandments of the Torah; and others believed 840, symbolic of fertility. Another analogy promoted their importance as fertility of the mind with thoughts on what is pure, lovely, and of good report. The last analogy resonates very much with these words from the Apostle Paul:

> *Finally, brothers and sisters, whatever is true, whatever is noble, whatever is right, whatever is pure, whatever is lovely, whatever is admirable—if anything is excellent or praiseworthy—think about such things. Whatever you have learned or received or heard from me, or seen in me— put it into practice. And the God of peace will be with you.*

(Philippians 4:8-9, NIV)

In Christian art, the pomegranate symbolizes the greatest gift of love: Christ's resurrection and its promise of eternal life and love – forever in heaven. Spanish missionaries brought pomegranate trees to the new world centuries ago. The real value of the fruit, however, was lost until very recently, when their sweet-tart taste and powerhouse of vitamins and antioxidants were rediscovered. "Poms" may help to support a healthy heart. The ruby red color is attributed to love, and usually the first one we choose to symbolize the heart.

Bathsheba proclaimed the noble woman's value far above rubies. All connected to love and God's love, Solomon elevated the ruby red pomegranate to top position. Not just heading the columns of the temple or his own head, it claimed the top spot of Solomon's Locked Garden. The very first fruit of the Spirit is Love.

Solomon declared that all the other fruits are the outgrowth of her branches – her Godly love courageously and lavishly shared with him and with others. The Apostle John confirms just how much God loves us and His desire for us to love one another.

> *Beloved, let us love one another, for love is from God; and everyone who loves is born of God and knows God. The one who does not love does not know God, for God is love. By this the love of God was manifested in us, that God has sent His only begotten Son into the world so that we might live through Him. In this is love, not that we loved God, but that He loved us and sent His Son to be the propitiation for our sins. Beloved, if God so loved us, we also ought to love one another. No one has seen God at any time; if we love one another, God abides in us, and His love is perfected in us. By this we know that we abide in Him and He in us, because He has given us of His Spirit. We have seen and testify that the Father has sent the Son to be the Savior of the world.*

(1 John 5:6-14, NASB)

The Apostle Paul wrote a whole chapter to the Corinthian church explaining what love is and is not. He ended the focus like this:

> *"Now these three remain: faith, hope, and love.*
> *But the greatest of these is love.*
> (1 Corinthians 13:13)

Solomon bookended his list with the two essences representing the Holy Spirit's fruit of love and of self-control. Self-control enables and encourages us in all the fruit in between – the ones that demonstrate our love for God and others. Reaching out in love to another requires courage to be vulnerable. Will we be loved in return? Will we be rejected? Will others scoff at

31

our well-intentioned acts of love? Solomon's bride held no exemption card. Kudos to Solomon, he looked for and exclaimed the very best in her, citing her, not just as an example of love, but of every single fruit growing in the Holy Spirit Garden.

Cutting open the pomegranate exposes its hundreds of seeds like ruby jewels of love. We can choose to keep them for ourselves, or share. Sharing produces returns on our investment, while hoarding leaves us wide open to egotistical and overindulgent behavior.

Fear and vulnerability threaten to paralyze our attempts to share our love. Sometimes we wonder what love might look like in a given situation. Like the pomegranate filled with seeds, the Holy Spirit fills our hearts with love – seeds of joy, peace, patience, kindness, goodness, gentleness, and faithfulness. His work in us, supplies us with courage to face life's realities head on. Possessing the fruit of self-control – sitting at the far end of the list, coupled with the fruit of love, ensures we are enabled to express and share the other fruit as the moment requires.

A Woman of the Bible Displays the Fruit

A Mother's Love

If you love something set it free.
If it comes back it was meant to be.
If it continues to fly let it soar, and have faith that
God has something better in store.
~~Anonymous

She released her baby, he was returned to her, and God planned something far better. Hers is one of the most beautiful stories of love in Scripture. Her name is Jochebed, the mother of Moses, and she loved pomegranates.

"Why did you bring us up out of Egypt to this terrible place?
It has no grain or figs, grapevines or pomegranates. . ."
(Numbers 20:5a, NIV)

The Israelites feasted in Egypt! They were slaves – brick makers – driven to the brink by cruel taskmasters, but they ate well, having all the fresh food they desired. That included pomegranates – this juicy crimson symbol of love. In spite of their harsh work environment, these people made time for their families, found energy to prepare amazing meals, and husbands and wives cherished their intimacy. Pharaoh (king of Egypt) wished it were not so, but these oppressed people produced fruit. God loved them and added to their numbers continuously. Pharaoh made a decision, taking Israelite population control into his own hands.

The king of Egypt said to the Hebrew midwives, whose names were Shiphrah and Puah, "When you are helping the Hebrew women during childbirth on the delivery stool, if you see that the baby is a boy, kill him; but if it is a girl, let her live." The midwives, however, feared God and did not do what the king of Egypt had told them to do; they let the boys live.

(Exodus 1:15-17, NIV)

Pharaoh's plan failed, and he found another way.

Then Pharaoh gave this order to all his people: "Every Hebrew boy that is born you must throw into the Nile, but let every girl live."

(Exodus 1:22, NIV)

Moses was born during this decree. We don't know how many mothers went to the great extent she did to protect their newborns during this time, but we know about Jochebed. For three months she hid Moses from Pharaoh's officials committed to sniffing out every dirty diaper and listening for every whimper of the Hebrews' baby boys. They came to carry out the Pharaoh's orders!

Jochebed was determined for Moses to live. When she could no longer hide him, she acted out of her great love for her baby boy. She carefully sealed the spaces of a covered basket. With her daughter, Miriam, posted at the lookout point, Jochebed courageously placed Moses in the basket, setting it afloat in the Nile near the king's palace.

"The woman became pregnant and gave birth to a son; when she saw that he was beautiful, she hid him for three months. But when she could no longer hide him, she got a papyrus basket for him and coated it with asphalt and pitch. She placed the child in it and set it among the reeds by the bank of the Nile. Then his sister (Miriam) stood at a distance in order to see what would happen to him."
(Exodus 2:2-4)

Pharaoh's daughter spotted the basket.

When she opened it, she saw the child—a little boy, crying. She felt sorry for him and said, "This is one of the Hebrew boys." Then his sister said to Pharaoh's daughter, "Should I go and call a woman from the Hebrews to nurse the boy for you?"
(Exodus 2:6-7)

Miriam intervened. Mom was hired to nurse and care for Moses. She received her baby right back, and she and her husband shared with all their children the wonderful history of God's work in their lives and the lives of their people. Her loving actions assured the continuation of God's love story. Moses grew up the son of a pagan princess; but he grew up learning his heritage and knowing God. The story of the Exodus revealed God's better plan, not just for Jochebed and her family, but also for Israel's future when God entrusted Moses to lead His people out of Egyptian slavery.

Seems Jochebed was prompted in her actions by Divine direction. The love she offered her infant son was the pure love of God living within her. Her name is the feminine form of Jehovah. She was undeniably created in His image.

Remember the robes adorned in pomegranates? Aaron, (Jochebed's middle child – also, her first-born son and big brother to Moses) wore the garment first. With God there are no coincidences or little things. God instructed Moses and Aaron to create and bring beautiful reminders of their mother's love (and a foreshadowing of what would come to symbolize Christ's resurrection with its promise of love and eternal life) right into the presence of Jehovah Himself.

We all desire to be loved by parents, siblings, spouse, children, and friends. No one will ever be able to love us like God loves us, or like He loved Jochebed, Moses or Miriam.

Has there been an occasion in your life where, like Jochebed, you had to let someone go, not knowing how that would turn out? It's really difficult, and demands much courage and even more, love. I know. I've been there. God directed my actions, and I prayed diligently for the outcome. It's been many years. The person passed away with no resolution. It still hurts. I'm looking forward to realizing God's better plan in this situation, when He and I finally meet face to face. Would you share your stories of letting go and letting God? Leave a post on our Facebook page to encourage others.

A little "food" for thought: Jochebed fed her family pomegranates. Make a quick search of the potential health benefits of pomegranates. [1] By eating them, they may have helped enrich her milk for Moses. Included in the family meal plan, pomegranates may have helped support the health of her whole household.

[1]Links to several different resources are found on this webpage:
Tohi, Willow, "History of Pomegranate," September 17, 2012, *Natural News*
http://www.naturalnews.com/042282_pomegranates_history_superfood.html

Pomegranate Essence Droplets

A wife of noble character who can find?
She is worth far more than rubies.
(Proverbs 31:10, NIV)

Fun Facts about Pomegranates

- The Spanish word for pomegranate is Granada. The city of Granada Spain, named for the fruit, uses a pomegranate in its coat of arms.[1]
- In the Hebrew Bible six fruits and grains are listed as native to Israel. Pomegranate is among the six.[2]
- The red seeds or the edible portion of the pomegranate, are also called arils. They may be very sweet or very tart, dependent on the fruit's ripeness.[3]
- Pomegranates are high in anti-oxidants, dietary fibers, vitamins A, C, and E, and other nutrients providing support for good health.[4]
- The Latin word for pomegranate means "apple with many seeds."[5]
- To some, the appearance of the pomegranate suggests a "petrified tomato."[6]
- Pomegranates contain three times as many antioxidants as either wine or green tea. [7]

Your turn

– Enjoy some Mulled Pomegranate Wine (non-alcoholic)

    2 cups pomegranate juice
    1 cup apple juice
    A pinch of cloves
    A pinch of cinnamon
    1 star anise
    1 medium orange
    1 small lemon
    Additional cinnamon sticks for garnish

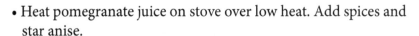

- Heat pomegranate juice on stove over low heat. Add spices and star anise.
- Zest lemon and orange, and add to the pomegranate mixture. Add the juice of the orange to the mixture.
- Simmer over low heat for 45 minutes.
- Using a mesh sieve, strain the juice into two mugs. Add a cinnamon stick to each mug.

– The recipe for Orange Pomegranate Scones is found on the menu board on our website. [8]

– Watch a video to see how to open a pomegranate.[9]

– Use fresh pomegranates in an autumn table arrangement.

– There are many pomegranate patterns for quilting and embroidery. Choose one you like and create:

- A quilt
- A table runner
- A set of coasters

– Pomegranate trees are among the best for a bonsai garden. Learn how at Bonsai Tree Care's website.[10]

[1] Cross, Sophie, "All hail the Pomegranate, official symbol of Granada," October 15, 2012, *The Lecrin Valley, https://thelecrinvalley.org/2012/10/15/all-hail-the-pomegranate-official-symbol-of-granada/*

[2] Moster, David, "Fruit in the Bible," September 29, 2016, *Bible History Daily, http://www.biblicalarchaeology.org/daily/ancient-cultures/daily-life-and-practice/fruit-in-the-bible/*

[3] French, Meredith, "Pomegranate the Crown Royal of All Fruit," Spring 2016, *Pacific Horticulture, http://www.pacifichorticulture.org/articles/pomegranate-2/*

[4] Bjorndal, Silje Mork, MS, RD, "Pomegranate the Antioxidant Powerhouse," *SuperKids Nutrition, http://www.superkidsnutrition.com/sf_pomegranate/*

[5] "Pomegranates," University of California Cooperative Extension, UCCE Maser Food Preservers of Orange County, *http://ucanr.edu/sites/MFPOC/Food_Preservation/Pomegranates/*

[6] "Pomegranates," University of California Cooperative Extension, UCCE Maser Food Preservers of Orange County, *http://ucanr.edu/sites/MFPOC/Food_Preservation/Pomegranates/*

[7] "7 Amazing Health Benefits of Pomegranate," *Organic Facts, https://www.organicfacts.net/health-benefits/fruit/health-benefits-of-pomegranate.html*

[8] www.LynnUWatson.com/cbs-menu

[9] "POMEGRANATE OPENING – Awesome Pomegranate Technique," FullHd-Nature (on YouTube), November 8, 2014, https://youtu.be/HGYpk395PUA

[10] Green, Mauricio, "What You Should Know about Caring for Your Pomegranate Bonsai," November 6, 2013, *Bonsai Tree Care – The Ultimate Guide, http://bonsaidude.com/know-caring-pomegranate-bonsai/*

Chapter 2

Henna - Joy

Cinnamah-Brosia and Friends

Share about Joy

Diffusing Today: Orange and Nutmeg essential oils

Aromatic influence: Citrus and nutmeg's sweet peaceful uplifting aroma that may help fill a room with a sense of peace, harmony, and creativity

Daily Delight: Chocolate Covered Peanut Butter Buttery Flavor Crackers

Musically: Happy Day (Tim Hughes)

Verse of the Day:
> *But I will sing of Your strength and will joyfully*
> *proclaim Your faithful love in the morning.*
> *For You have been a stronghold for me,*
> *a refuge in my day of trouble.*
> (Psalm 59:16)

She was late. The past eight weeks I could set my clock by her arrival. Autumn had been unseasonably warm, and Sara seated herself in the wooden rocker on the cafe's back porch at precisely 8:45 each morning, her order always the same. I welcomed her with black coffee and an orange pomegranate scone. Except for a simple and unenthusiastic "thank you," she rarely spoke. She stared at the gardens for an hour before slipping back out. Her sadness haunted me. That day her absence haunted me even more.

No one knew how to find her or check on her. The last customers of the day had left two hours earlier. I just finished the day's cleanup when, disheveled and dragging her feet, Sara knocked at the door. I let her in, poured us coffee, and we walked to the garden. Our feet dangled from the swing, and Sara began to share.

 "My mom had been very sick. She died six months ago. My world fell apart. I moved here to run away from my pain. Sitting here enjoying the fresh scent of the garden became my refuge. I would just stare at the garden and attempt to rock my woes away. Cinnamah-Brosia, Mom was always so full of joy and sunshine. She told me it was because of Jesus. Growing up, He wasn't part of our lives. After the abuse she and I had endured from my father, I just knew her new friend was a fantasy tale. You're always so happy and joyful, like she was. I'm hoping maybe you can help me."

"Sara, I wish I showed that joy all the time, but I often fall short. Let me tell you about a time early this year your mom's friend – and mine – had to remind me about joy. It's not about you or me or about our feelings. It's about being in His presence every moment of every day.

"First it was the espresso machine. We purchased a second-hand machine, which faithfully steamed up espresso for a few years. On this particular morning, however, it was done! Then, a tray of dishes slid from my hand – broken pieces everywhere! As my nerves and behavior unraveled, Jane – always-joyful Jane – came through the door. Jumping right in, she helped clear the mess. While I muttered and complained under my breath, I continued preparing goodies for our customers. Jane promised to shop for a new espresso machine.

"The phone call came that same day almost a year ago now. Gram had just been admitted to ICU. Her neighbor found her sitting on her porch. Something was terribly wrong. She had suffered a stroke. My joy fizzled faster than the air out of a long balloon. I felt my life spiraling out of control even faster. Mom had circled her hippie-mobile in and out of my life as a child. Our family lived our joyless, dysfunctional life in another town. I loved visiting here and spending summers with Gram and Gramps. Gram always had the right words, and she loved me unconditionally. Jeremy and I married and moved away. Years later, we moved our family back here, partially for me to help Gram with the café. She and I worked side by side for several more years. She retired from the day-to-day operations almost two years ago, but she always checked in. That morning there was no word from her at all. Caught up in my problems, I had not even noticed. Now, she needed me at the hospital, and I was emotionally unavailable. All the mess of the day had blackened my attitude. Tears spilled everywhere. How would I put on a happy face for this joy-filled woman who loved me so much all the time?

"Wiping the smudges away as best I could, I headed for the hospital, while Jane took care of our guests. Gram looked lovingly into my eyes once more before hers closed for the last time. I slowly walked off with the negative thought patrol marching formations around my head. I was kicking things, blaming myself and others. I screamed about my anger toward Mom for being so rebellious with my grandparents. Life was pretty much over at that moment. Some may have witnessed my fits, but I doubted any cared. Many of those thoughts are similar to yours right now, I bet."

Amidst sobs, Sara blubbered, "You got me on that one! But how did you ever get through the pain, Cinnamah-Brosia?"

"Sara, are you willing to consider that your mom may have been telling you the truth about Jesus? Would you allow me to share a precious encounter with her friend? It was just a couple weeks later in this garden."

"Go ahead. At this point I doubt I'll want to meet Him, but I asked. I may not like what you have to say, but I'm listening."

"Each morning before friends gather at the coffee cottage, Jesus and I sip our coffee together out here in the garden. It keeps me calm and refreshes my joy. After Gram passed away, I decided extra time communing with my pillow was worth far more than time spent with Jesus. An urgent nudge to go to the garden interrupted my sleep very early one morning several weeks later. I reluctantly submitted. Birds were chirping while squirrels were skittering. Dew was still on the ground. I walked among the spring flowers. I surprised myself that I noticed their fragrance.

"I knew Jesus was reminding me that Gram's joy came from Him. He gently encouraged, 'Cinnamah-B, Gram and I spent time out here each morning, too. I guided her into her day with joy no matter what tangled mess tugged on her life.' Jesus wrapped His arm around my shoulder. He spoke softly, but I heard him clearly: 'It's how Gram kept joyful tunes in her heart. That's been your refuge, too.'

"He was right, of course. I had found an excuse to skip our time that day, too. What a great friend to come nudge me out of bed. While I was thanking Him for that, an old hymn came to mind. He and I sang the hymn together. I think I heard Gram's voice joining in. I was smiling again – in the midst of my loss."

I come to the garden alone,
While the dew is still on the roses;
And the voice I hear, falling on my ear,
The Son of God discloses.

And he walks with me, and he talks with me,
And he tells me I am his own,
And the joy we share as we tarry there,
None other has ever known.

He speaks, and the sound of his voice
Is so sweet the birds hush their singing;
And the melody that he gave to me
Within my heart is ringing.

And he walks with me, and he talks with me,
And he tells me I am his own,
And the joy we share as we tarry there,
None other has ever known.

I'd stay in the garden with him
Tho the night around me be falling;
But he bids me go; thro' the voice of woe,
His voice to me is calling.

And he walks with me, and he talks with me,
And he tells me I am his own,
And the joy we share as we tarry there,
None other has ever known. [1]

"Does that sound like the joy your mom experienced, Sara? Jesus is waiting to be your friend, too. Maybe you found the garden such a great escape, because you felt what you couldn't explain. Our ladies' group meets at the cottage every Tuesday evening. Will you join us? Jane will be here. She leads our Bible study and never misses. We always have room for one more, and we always leave a seat for Jesus. I know He's going to be so excited to see you."

What about you, precious reader? Are you plugged into a small group that loves each other and loves Jesus? If not, please ask a Jesus-following friend if you can join her and her friends, or contact a local Bible believing church – I pray for the warm welcome they extend. To my Jesus-follower friends reading this, please be observant of those around you. Look for the one in need of an invitation. It's so true that many do not know Jesus and do not attend church, Bible studies or small groups because no one has asked them. Who will you bring along?

[1]Miles, Charles Austin, *In the Garden*, 1912 (Public Domain)

The Essence of Henna in Scripture
Under the Henna Bush with Jesus

*Botanical name: Lawsonia Inermis; decorative paste made from
the leaves (in ancient tradition, it was mixed with sandalwood oil);
native to North Africa*

They conspicuously stand out in the crowd. Redheads make up less than two percent of the world's population. Many more folks derive fiery tresses from a box. Henna's natural red color has made it popular for 1000's of years for hair dye – one solution to an individual's desire to be noticed.

The color red stands out boldly in the world's sea of predominantly dark-haired individuals. It also pops boldly off a black background, appearing to be larger than life.

An ages old tradition involving a tray of henna has much in common with another tradition that first began with a parasol of gifts. Invitations for both request the presence of the bride's female friends and family members. The celebration of great joy occurs a short time before the wedding and nearly always boasts the essential fancy foods and decorations.

A parasol of small gifts opened over the bride's head (think confetti rain here) launched the bridal shower tradition as we know it in the United States. Over the years, other traditions were added to the party – like larger gifts often fancily wrapped. One claim asserted breaking a few ribbons on these gifts meant a few babies for the couple – a baby for each broken ribbon.

The cultural tradition of the henna ceremony in the Middle East and other Asian and African countries brings the bride's female friends and family members together with a tray of henna paste, dancing, and celebrating. The henna tray travels to the bride and the others in turn. The ladies paint fancy and often elaborate designs on each other's hands and feet. Custom suggests the henna may encourage blossoming new life for the nuptial couple.

While the "baby" part of both celebrations is likely more conjecture than fact, both are joyous merry making occasions, celebrating the love of the bride and her groom.

Henna paste is made from the leaves of the henna plant. The flowers exude a tantalizing sweet and slightly earthy aroma. The essence may have lured Solomon and his bride to tuck themselves underneath the henna bush catching the fragrance along with moments of intimacy. Intimate love is joyous and worthy of the celebration.

Henna represents joy as fruit of the Spirit. In times of great celebration like a wedding, joy overflows. What about those dark moments of trouble in our lives? The perfection of our faith depends on having joy – especially in those moments. When our reactions look different than the expected response under the weight of our trials, we stand out in the crowd. Our joy is red-on-black conspicuous. Others gaze on us in amazement, wondering if they can duplicate our look from a box. It's our moment to shine the reason for our joy, and God receives the glory!

From his bride we hear these words about Solomon:
My love is a cluster of henna blossoms to me,
(Song of Solomon 1:14)

Solomon says of his bride:
Your branches are a paradise of pomegranates
with choicest fruits, henna with nard—
(Song of Solomon 4:13)

Their love exuded joy. The beauty of their intimacy stemmed from loving God first and finding joy in His presence. The couple knew each other well. They took the opportunity to observe their love in happy times and under stress-filled circumstances. Gifting each other with this imagery, the joy they evidenced in each other displayed more than a lover's moment of bliss.

Does joy conspicuously bubble up in you no matter what you are facing? Is there evidence you spend time with Jesus under the henna bush?

"You reveal the path of life to me; in Your presence is abundant joy; in Your right hand are eternal pleasures."
(Psalm 16:11)

If this fruit is lacking in your life, what steps are you willing to take to allow God to gift you His eternal pleasures, and the Holy Spirit to pour abundant joy into your harvest? Time in the Word is definitely time "in His presence." Begin with a Bible word search on "joy." While only three references to henna appear in Scripture, all in Song of Solomon, 242 verses proclaim joy!

How do you celebrate your joy? Henna art closely resembles designs seen in adult coloring books. That activity is a joyful one for many. Color and frame this tree as a reminder of the Holy Spirit fruit: JOY![1]

[1]Author holds copyright to this artwork. Permission is granted to copy and enlarge for your personal use.

The henna ceremony/celebration was neither embraced nor forbidden by Jewish laws, and was being culturally practiced in the Middle East and North Africa at the time of Solomon. Henna's fragrance and/or its cosmetic use provided a joyous experience. While tattooing is controversial, henna designs do not pierce the skin, they are not permanent, and are unrelated to Leviticus 19:28. They would not be a breach of traditional laws and teachings against actual tattoos. [1]

[1] "Permitted Tattoos," May 5, 2011, Traveling Rabbi.com, http://travelingrabbi.com/jewish-travel/permitted-tattoos

Choose Joy – Elizabeth Did

I've got the joy, joy, joy, joy, down in my heart,
down in my heart to stay.
(Children's Hymn)[1]

Fifteen teens and one mom driving us in her little VW bug, picking up donut holes. That's the number I remember, but that was fifty years ago. Every morning we packed ourselves into that little car like clowns at the circus. Our adventures ensured snacks for Vacation Bible School that week. And, yes, we went into the bakery together to pick them up. Everyone crawled back in, finding room for the boxes of donut holes, too.

This moment of joy was so insignificant, yet it still brings a smile to my face every time I think of it. My little memory lives in my heart (and maybe that of the other dozen or so involved in that escapade). Luke recorded Elizabeth's joy in His gospel – for *all* time.

When Elizabeth heard Mary's greeting, the baby leaped in her womb; and Elizabeth was filled with the Holy Spirit. And she cried out with a loud voice and said, "Blessed are you among women, and blessed is the fruit of your womb! And how has it happened to me, that the mother of my Lord would come to me? For behold, when the sound of your greeting reached my ears, the baby leaped in my womb for joy. And blessed is she who believed that there would be a fulfillment of what had been spoken to her by the Lord."
(Luke 1:40-45, NASB)

Confirming life begins at conception, little John jumped up and down in his mommy's womb. He recognized His Savior at that very moment, and greeted Him with joy and excitement. Elizabeth knew her God and knew His promises. She, too, recognized her Savior before His birth. The recognition rewarded her with great joy even among the sorrows of her life.

Elizabeth, advanced in years, became pregnant with Jesus' cousin, John. This would be her first – and as far as we know – only child. An angel foretold the birth in quite amazing fashion. John's dad, Zacharias, was a priest in the temple. The angel spoke to him as he was burning incense there. Listen to the angel's words:

> But the angel said to him: "Do not be afraid, Zechariah; your prayer has been heard. Your wife Elizabeth will bear you a son, and you are to call him John. He will be a joy and delight to you, and many will rejoice because of his birth,"
>
> (Luke 1:12-14, NIV)

The promise alone brought significant joy to this couple. And the mother of her Lord visited her while they were both with child. Her mind certainly entertained this verse often during those days:

> The Lord your God is in your midst, a victorious warrior.
> He will exult over you with joy, He will be quiet in His love,
> He will rejoice over you with shouts of joy.
> (Zephaniah 3:17, NASB)

Elizabeth's struggles furnished ample reason to whine about her circumstances. For years she lived through the pain of barrenness. She would struggle with caring for a tiny infant at her advanced age. Mary traveled to visit her. Had a move separated the family? Transportation wasn't a short drive in the family car or a quick plane hop away. She sure couldn't pick up the phone and call. Adding further to her struggles, during her pregnancy those who knew Elizabeth questioned her wisdom about the choice of a name for the baby. The angel announced the child's name to Zacharias. Because of his unbelief, God chose to mute him until John was born. Only at John's birth was he able to confirm her choice. Still she chose joy.

Dr. Wess Stafford knows a bit about choosing joy. He's chosen it against the odds in his own life. Leading Compassion International for many years, he saw many of the world's poorest families choose joy. He's shared about it in his book, *Too Small to Ignore.*

"Joy is a decision, a really brave one,
about how you are going to respond to life."[2]

Did Elizabeth have a henna ceremony when she and Zacharias tied the knot? Did her friends get together to bless her in their new beginning? Did Mary's friends gather for the henna celebration when she and Joseph finally married after the birth of this great big bundle of joy named Jesus? Those facts remain a mystery, but all the henna in the world will never surpass the joy Jesus brings to the lives of those who believe on His name and make Him Lord of their lives.

[1] Cooke, George Willis, *I've Got That Joy Joy Joy Joy,* date unknown, (Public Domain)

[2] Stafford, Dr. Wes with Merrill, Dean, *Too Small to Ignore: Why the Least of These Matters Most,* Special Edition, (Waterbrook Press, 12265 Oracle Boulevard, Colorado Springs, Copyright 2007) page 165

Henna Essence Droplets

Strength and honor are her clothing,
and she can laugh at the time to come.
(Proverbs 31:25)

Fun Facts about Henna

- The henna plant is the sole species in the Lawsonia genus. [1]
- Henna designs last one to four weeks on the hands.[2]
- Tradition says the bride is not permitted to do any housework until the bridal henna pattern has faded away. It may have been an excuse for an extended honeymoon, too. [3]
- Henna has been used for hair coloring and makeup for more than 3,000+ years. [4] A contemporary quote from Anne Lamott says, "Joy is the best makeup." [5] They were on to something all those centuries ago.
- In some cultures where the henna ceremony is practiced, it is the tradition to carefully hide the groom's initials in the elaborate designs. After the wedding, he looks for them.[6]
- The henna ceremony was considered symbolic of the couple's love and love shared between their families.[7]
- Around 200 A.D. henna was recognized as an agricultural product of Israel and became subject to tithing.[8]
- The Russian word for "red" is beautiful. [9]

Your turn

– Henna can be grown as a houseplant. Learn how to do it. [10]

– Create a collage or a "wall of joy." Use Scripture verses with the word joy (remember there are 242 to choose from). Do an internet search for quotes about joy.

– Use icing to decorate cookies with henna-style designs.

– Paint henna designs around a candle.

– Embroider or machine embroider henna-style designs on clothing, bags, pillows, etc.

 – Henna kits are available for you to try your hand at the art. If unavailable at your local craft supply, an internet search should help you locate one. WARNING: Some people have severe allergic reactions to henna. Please test the henna dye on a very small patch of skin first.

[1] "About Henna," *Silk & Stone, http://silknstone.com/About-Henna.html*

[2] "About Henna," *Silk & Stone, http://silknstone.com/About-Henna.html*

[3] "About Henna," *Silk & Stone, http://silknstone.com/About-Henna.html*

[4] Rennells, Lauren, "Henna as Hair Color, A History and Caution," July 18, 2009, *Bobby Pin Blog at Vintage Hairstyling. com http://www.vintagehairstyling. com/bobbypinblog/2009/07/henna-as-hair-color-a-history-and-caution.html*

[5] Lamott, Anne, *Grace (Eventually): Thoughts on Faith*, (Riverhead Press, New York, 2007), page 77

[6] Jones, Paula, "Some Interesting Facts About Henna," October 10, 2006, *Confetti, http://www.confetti.co.uk/wedding-ceremonies/some-interesting-facts-about-henna*

[7] Jones, Paula, "Some Interesting Facts About Henna," October 10, 2006, *Confetti, http://www.confetti.co.uk/wedding-ceremonies/some-interesting-facts-about-henna*

[8] Hakofer, Eshkol, "What Would Jesus Do (About Henna)? The Place of Henna in Ancient and Modern Christianity," June 5, 2014, *http://eshkolhakofer.blogspot. com/2014/06/what-would-jesus-do-about-henna-place.html*

[9] Kubilius, Kerry, "Red in Russian Culture: The Color Red is Beautiful in Russian Language," *about travel, http://goeasteurope.about.com/od/russia/a/ Russian-Culture-Facts.html*

[10] "How to Grow Henna," *wikiHow to do anything, http://www.wikihow.com/ Grow-Henna*

Chapter 3

Spikenard - Peace

Cinnamah-Brosia and Friends
Share about Peace

Diffusing Today: Spikenard and Lavender

Aromatic Influence: These outdoorsy and floral aromas may help provide a spiritually uplifting and peaceful feeling in the room.

Daily Delight: Cherry Crumb Coffee Cake

Musically: You Lift Me Up (Celtic Women)

Verse of the Day:

> The Lord will give strength to His people;
> The Lord will bless His people with peace.
> (Psalm 29:11, NASB)

"Jesus' peace. It fell on me like a warm velvet robe in the ER waiting room and never left. I knew where Ben was going when he died. He didn't always believe, but many years ago – your mom was a teenager then – God gave your Gramps a second chance, and he'd taken it. God will take care of me. I have His peace and His joy," she assured me.

I'll never forget those words the day Gramps passed on to be with Jesus. I had only known him as the kindly man that bounced me on his knee, taught me to fish and grow tomatoes, caught lightening bugs with me, and read stories to me before Gram tucked me in on summer nights. I missed him terribly, but not nearly as much as I knew she would. Everything in Gram's life was changing. There would be storms ahead, but she kept her voice lifted in praise:

I love Thee because Thou hast first loved me,
And purchased my pardon on Calvary's tree;
I love Thee for wearing the thorns on Thy brow; [1]

That was fifteen years ago. Gram kept the café open. It would keep her focus on others instead of her new reality – life without the man she had loved for fifty years. Gram still had lots of spunk, but a little help to keep it all running smoothly was essential.

Jeremy and I faced a crossroads in our life, with few prospects. We chose to come "home." Jeremy joined his dad in his business. Their new partnership blessed both of them and our whole family. Gram delighted in my assistance to continue the work she loved.

My own children grew up spending lots of time hanging out here, experiencing Gram's kindness and gentleness like I had. I watched her manage well, overcoming her fears with unexplainable peace and joy every day. Her gift of encouragement flowed freely and blessed many.

I was sharing all this with our Tuesday night group shortly after my own daughter and I had renovated and reopened as Cinnamah-Brosia's Coffee Cottage and Gift Shop. Most of the ladies had been regulars here since childhood. All listened intently as, one by one, the ladies shared their stories of Gram's peaceful spirit affecting their lives. Carol went first.

"When we lost our baby at just two months old, Miss Dot crocheted a blanket to wrap her tiny body. Tucked inside her soft and cuddly handiwork was a silver cross with a Scripture attached. I treasure it dearly."

The Lord is close to the brokenhearted
and saves those who are crushed in spirit.
(Psalm 34:18, NIV)

Melanie spoke up next. "My parents and I really clashed on so many things when I was a teen – that might be an understatement. Miss Dot believed in me when I believed no one else did. I accepted her invitation to help here after school. As we worked, she shared her own challenges as a young woman. She encouraged me to align my choices with God's Word and obey my parents. There's a special Scripture she gave me, too. 'Focus on the promise of this Word and living it, too; and blessings of joy and peace will abound in your life,' she said. She was right."

> *Children, do what your parents tell you. This is only right.*
> *"Honor your father and mother" is the first commandment*
> *that has a promise attached to it, namely, so you will live*
> *well and have a long life.*
> (Ephesians 6:1-3, MSG)

Gram believed God: she and her family were doubly clothed. Their physical needs were met. She prayed a spiritual cover over them every day, then shared Jesus every chance she found. Countless times she spoke the words of the Peacemaker, and lives changed. I'm sure she claimed this promise often:

> *Peace I leave with you. My peace I give to you.*
> *I do not give to you as the world gives.*
> *Your heart must not be troubled or fearful.*
> (John 14:26-28, HCSB)

With fear and trembling rather than tranquility in our hearts, it's challenging to find courage to make a difference for others. Many broken lives await Jesus' peace and a touch of kindness. Our little group knelt together in prayer.

Father God – giver of every perfect gift, help us hold each other accountable. Open our eyes to the people around us desperate for Your touch. Give us courage and boldness to offer Your love, not knowing the reception our words and deeds will receive. Cover our families with Your peace just like Miss Dot's warm, velvet robe. Let it invade our own stress. Enable us to reach out in the practical and kind ways, the same as Miss Dot always did . . .

So quiet except for tears, until one voice broke the silence and we all joined in.

My Jesus I love Thee....[2]

[1]Featherston, William R., My Jesus I Love Thee, 1864, (Public Domain)

[2]Featherston, William R., My Jesus I Love Thee, 1864, (Public Domain)

The Essence of Spikenard in Scripture

What is Your Spikenard?

Botanical name: Nardostachys jatamansi;
fragrant oil steam-distilled from the roots; native to India

"Ewww.... that smells like my closet floor with all my dirty clothes and smelly socks!" That was one young lady's spontaneous reaction as my husband shared spikenard with his fifth grade Sunday school class. The day's lesson: Mary anointing Jesus' head. We can be sure the aroma of a full pint of the oil filled the room. Shooey!!!

The cost – not the aroma – alarmed the disciples (especially Judas, the one who later betrayed Him for personal financial gain). The others' concerns acknowledged the fact spikenard sold for a handsome price, and the money could help the poor. There was surely a better use for the resource than pouring a whole pint of expensive oil on someone's head.

Considering the cost and undeterred by their criticism, razzing and complaints, Mary chose to serve Jesus. She believed He was the most valuable investment opportunity in her life. Hindsight tells us she was absolutely correct!

Using spikenard for its comforting and calming scent and its potentially helpful topical support for healthy-looking skin was common first century practice. Passover was just two days away. Jesus was quickly approaching His death and resurrection. Prophets foretold the deep stress and painful wounds he faced.

But he was pierced for our transgressions, he was crushed
for our iniquities; the punishment that brought us peace
was on him, and by his wounds we are healed.
(Isaiah 53:5, NIV)

Mary may have known Scriptures foretelling the abuse he would face, but she would not have made the imminent connection. Jesus Himself recognized exactly what lay ahead. He assured them, *"By pouring this fragrant oil on My body, she has prepared Me for burial."* (Matthew 26:12)

A pint of pure 'nard' represented a year's wages for a common worker. For a woman of ill repute, it was her life and livelihood. Recognizing her unworthiness and seeing Him as The Priceless Treasure worth seeking at any cost, Mary gave everything to the One who was about to give His life for her.

> *"By pouring this fragrant oil on My body,*
> *she has prepared Me for burial. I assure you: Wherever this*
> *gospel is proclaimed in the whole world, what this*
> *woman has done will also be told in memory of her."*
> (Matthew 26:12, 13) See also: Mark 14:3-9

Breaking open that full jar of oil would have contributed to a peaceful atmosphere for all that were present. Considering the conflict that arose, Mary may have been the subject of the controversy in this scene, but she may well have provided the antidote too.

Centuries earlier Solomon observed, noted, and experienced the fruit of an intimate relationship with God in the life of his bride and included spikenard – an aroma of peace and calming – in his garden descriptive.

When serving others, you lead with your heart. The act of serving is known to reduce stress and mild depression, and even make us happier. That sounds like a recipe for greater peace in our lives; and serving the poor, the naked, the stranger in need is seeing and serving Jesus. Serving is many times smelly at best. When we recognize our unworthiness, we see Jesus as The Priceless Treasure worth the cost and the stench. What is your spikenard? What represents your life and a huge sacrifice if asked to pour it out for Jesus? Knowing your future may be affected and/or your action may draw heavy criticism, could you do it? Would you find the courage to do it? Do you see how, like Mary, your actions could bring much needed peace in that moment?

A Woman of the Bible Displays the Fruit

The Lady with the Peace Symbol

Peace is a belief that exhales. Because you believe that God's provision is everywhere – like air. [1]
~~Ann Voskamp

Peace symbols everywhere . . .the sign of the times! That symbol made its debut in 1958. Very young children then, but as teens in the late 1960s the boomers (my generation) embraced the upside down "Y" and the two-finger greeting. We searched for elusive peace in all the wrong places. The symbol became as familiar as the school bell signaling the start of a new day. We longed for a new day of peace.

The Vietnam Conflict (never officially declared a war) raged on and on. The three big networks' six and ten o'clock electronic scrapbooks broadcast this unpopular battle into our homes every evening. The United States alone lost 58,220 lives. Thousands more were seriously injured. These were our siblings and friends. A tumbler bearing the theme of the day – "War is not healthy for children and other living things" – is all that remains of my personal artifacts. It holds pens, pencils, and a few strange memories as it keeps silent watch on my desk.

The peace symbol recently emerged in a huge comeback. I asked my grandchildren what history they knew of that sign they loved to draw and wear. Not much, but their generation is in need of peace, too. Wars, on one stage or another, from domestic to global in scope, rage on today. Their lives and ours are affected.

The symbol's history dates back to the early days of the nuclear war threats.[2] Theories exist of roots in some heathen rituals as well. The concept of peace and the desire for peace were not new as the boomer generation came of age, and it's not new today. Peace is elusive, and the sign is just a sign. It attracts attention, but doesn't end war and conflict. Unrest entered the world with Adam and Eve's sinful choice in the garden. It intensified when their son, Cain, murdered his brother, Abel. *War and Peace* claims high ranking on the list of longest novels ever written. Wars have punctuated all of mortal history, and they will until Jesus comes back for His bride.

Deborah, one of the greatest peacemakers in all of Scripture, knew a thing or two about war and peace! A prophetess, wife of Lappidoth, and a judge in Israel, Deborah regularly communed with God. She shared the wisdom He entrusted to her. As God directed, she summoned Israelite military leader, Barak, with these words:

> *"Hasn't the Lord the God of Israel, commanded you: 'Go deploy the troops on Mount Tabor, and take with you 10,000 men from the Naphtalites and Zebulunites. Then I will lure Sisera commander of Jabin's forces, his chariots, and his army at the Wadi Kishon to fight against you, and I will hand him over to you.'"*

(Judges 4:6-7)

Hesitant Barak would only go if Deborah went, too. Really? The request surely gained this lily-liver a royal roasting around the campfire for many years to come. Whatever grief this decision earned him, Deborah agreed to go. God warned Barak through her:

> *"I will go with you," she said, "but you will receive no honor on the road you are about to take, because the Lord will sell Sisera into a woman's hand."*

(Judges 4:9)

Deborah delivered the orders. She, Barak, and the army moved forward. Not one of Sisera's men was left – only Sisera. True to Deborah's words of warning from the Lord, Sisera himself fell at the hands of a woman. This scaredy cat ran to a home he believed safe. Jael greeted him, invited him in, and played the most gracious hostess. When he fell asleep – boom, he was dead! She nailed a tent peg right through his head!

Barak worried about the instructions he received from God. The odds were poor, and he lacked trust for a good outcome. Deborah knew no worry at all. She prayed. God spoke to her clearly. She trusted His guidance, and responded with courage. Deborah's calm in the midst of the storm and Jael's quick thinking landed this Israeli battle in the victory column with a capital V.

> *Don't worry about anything, but in everything, through prayer and petition with thanksgiving, let your requests be made known to God. And the peace of God, which surpasses every thought, will guard your hearts and minds in Christ Jesus.*
> (Philippians 4:6-7)

There was great joy in Israel that day in answer to Deborah's prayers! Centuries later Jesus – same yesterday, today, and tomorrow – would make this promise:

> *Until now you have asked for nothing in My name;*
> *ask and you will receive, so that your joy may be made full.*
> (John 16:24, NASB)

In Philippians, Paul instructed that making our requests known to God brings peace. Where we have peace, we also have joy. The Greek word used to tell us the peaceful fragrance of Mary's spikenard "filled" the room is the same Greek word Jesus used to tell us that, through our communication and relationship with Him, our joy would be made "full."

Deborah and Barak's full joy in God's victory spilled over as they sang and praised Him for the full 31 verses of Judges 5. The chapter closes, "And the land was peaceful 40 years.

Not just wars, but personal struggles, relationship challenges, family disputes, corporate politics, church disagreements, neighborhood battles, and more complicate our lives every day. Are you more likely to be a part of the peaceful solution when you find yourself in struggles like these, or do your actions add to the drama? God desires for our lives to be joyful, because peace then resides in our hearts. When you see a peace symbol, think of spikenard; inhale its earthy scent. Ask Jesus to go in front of you and behind you. The victory is His, and an eternity of peace awaits you.

[1] Voskamp, Ann, *Unwrapping the Greatest Gift: A Family Celebration of Christmas*, (Carol Stream, Illinois: Tyndale House Publishers, 2014) page 44.

[2] "The Origin of the Peace Symbol: A History of the Campaign for Nuclear Disarmament (CND) Logo," Docs Populi, *http://www.docspopuli.org/articles/PeaceSymbolArticle.html*

Spikenard Essence Droplets

She is not afraid for her household when it snows,
for all in her household are doubly clothed.
(Proverbs 31:21)

Fun Facts about Spikenard

- Spikenard has become an endangered species. It is often harvested with little consideration for proper steps to assure its sustainability. [1]
- May be found growing wild on a stony or grassy slope. [2]
- Pope Francis incorporated spikenard into his coat of arms.[3]
- The entire plant is very fragrant, which is spikenard's defensive system to fight bacteria and insects.
- It was common in Biblical times to preserve spikenard in an alabaster box. Mary brought it exactly this way when she anointed Jesus feet.
- Spikenard essential oil is very thick. Colors range from amber to green to deep blue. Green is considered higher quality. [4]
- Humility™, a proprietary blend from Young Living Essential Oils™, contains spikenard. Without humility there is little peace.

Your turn

– The lyrics of the song *"Alabaster Box"* (CeCe Winans) beautifully portray the peace that surpasses understanding, poured out with the spikenard in Mary's alabaster box. Use your search engine to find the lyrics to this song. Download it from your music app store. Or perhaps it's already in your collection. Take the time to listen, and be refreshed in the powerful message.

– Mix spikenard and lavender essential oils with aloe Vera for an after sun spray. Use approximately 2 ounces aloe Vera gel, 10-12 drops of lavender, and 2-3 drops of spikenard.

– Diffuse spikenard essential oil coupled with another oil or two of your choice. Spikenard blends well with lavender, cistus, patchouli, pine, and vetiver.

– Find a pint container of your choice to represent an alabaster box. Fill it with Scriptures and sayings about peace. When you or your friend needs encouragement, these inspirational notes will be at your fingertips.

[1] "Spikenard," *Only Foods, http://www.onlyfoods.net/spikenard.html*

[2] "Spikenard," *Only Foods, http://www.onlyfoods.net/spikenard.html*

[3] The Coat of Arms of Pope Francis, *Libreria Editrice Vaticana,*

https://w2.vatican.va/content/francesco/en/elezione/stemma-papa-francesco.html

[4] "Spikenard Organic Essential Oil," *Victorie, Inc., http://www.victorie-inc.us/ spikenard.html*

Chapter 4

Saffron - Patience

Share About Patience

Diffusing Today: Bergamot and Lavender essential oils

Aromatic Influence: This combination of herbaceous lemony and floral aromas may help fill the room with a sense of peacefulness and confidence

Daily Delight: Biscuits with Saffron Vanilla Honey

Musically: Cast My Cares (Finding Favour)

Verse of the Day:

> *But if we hope for what we do not see,*
> *we eagerly wait for it with patience.*
> (Romans 8:25)

While the coffee cottage was being renovated and through several delays, our small group continued to meet in the construction zone. With a projected completion date less than two weeks away, Jane challenged us to bring a "patience" lesson the next week. Hear the groans?

Jeremy and I learned big lessons in patience years earlier. They were invaluable when one challenge after another presented itself. Those house-flipping shows teach old homes and new codes don't mix. Keeping vintage character while adding modern conveniences had kept us on collision highway. Gram and Kaitlyn's plan for the makeover

was fabulous. Doing the work on our own allowed the money Gram left for the project to go much further, but our adventure in renovation took on a life of its own. We navigated with unexpected patience, and I knew why.

We married as soon as we could after finishing school. It was 1990. We moved away to a bigger city. Jeremy had a great job in the blossoming technology field. We quickly established our careers. We were set! We wanted a family, too. Why not go for it? Two years later our careers continued advancing without a baby in the picture.

Our faith, once very much alive, simmered on lukewarm. We prayed those "gimme" prayers asking for a baby. We had never given our dream to God. Regular pew warmers, we heard Pastor Rick teach about Abraham obeying God – laying his dream, his firstborn child, Isaac – on the altar. Abraham trusted God for the best plan. And He delivered. Moved by Abraham and Isaac's experience – a huge lesson in faith and patience – we approached the altar and humbly placed our baby dream in His hands, and trusted for a miracle. The week before, a doctor had assured us our ability to conceive was close to nil.

We agreed during our dating days, adoption would be a part of our family plan. Monday morning we jumped on it. This would be a challenge, too. Age restrictions hampered our options. Surprised beyond measure, Thursday that week we discovered I was pregnant! Kaitlyn was born November 10, 1994.

Two short months later, Jeremy's cousin, Samantha, presented a huge request. She was 16, pregnant, devastated, and desired for her baby what she couldn't possibly provide. The father encouraged her to abort. Broken-hearted, she asked us to adopt her child. Aaron arrived in May of 1995. We welcomed the baby into our family. He and Samantha have a beautiful relationship, too. And our surprise bundle of joy, Caryn, was born in November 1998.

All we endured prior to our move back to Pearlville required amazing patience and courage as well. How could we not trust God in all the details of the coffee cottage project, even with all of the delays? This particular Tuesday Bible study rolled around quickly. It had been six months since we began the renovations, but Friday morning Miss Dot's Café had finally reopened as Cinnamah-Brosia's Coffee Cottage and Gift Shop. Jane, Kaitlyn and I prayed together before the ladies arrived. Their patience stories gleaned from Life University awaited us all.

"Craig and I wanted that house so badly," Jennifer reminisced. "It was just perfect. A bidding war began. Finally, another couple wrote a contract way over the asking price. Our dreams sank. Two more years crawled by before we found another house that grand and affordable. I'm grateful God answered, 'wait,' to our prayers on that one. We learned contentment where we were. When the first house burned due to an overlooked electrical problem, I felt so badly for the family that purchased it, but I also knew God had protected us."

Susan remembered, "We were so poor when Mark and I married. The long promised pay raise never materialized. I walked down the street to my fast food job – the only one I could find at the time. It paid very little, and what a waste of my degree. Melissa's bookstore would open next month on the other end of town. Mark's mom lived next door to Melissa and knew all about it. Melissa needed an assistant manager. It was too good to be true, but I landed and accepted the position . . . with no transportation options. One car provided all we had needed until then. Mark and I prayed and looked at cars all week. The price tag on anything reliable registered way out of our reach. With only a few days until I started the new job, I broke down in tears. Sobbing, I answered Mom's call. Mark and I had talked to God about the challenge, but had left mom out of our problem. Speechless is all I can say of my reaction to her news. They had just purchased a new car. She wanted me to have her old one. Old meant four years old and perfectly well maintained. No strings attached. They were already on the road delivering it."

Tears of joy flooded the place as we shared how God was building our courage to trust patiently for His best. We cheered the opening of Cinnamah-Brosia's Coffee Cottage and Gift Shop, and thanked Him for the memories of Miss Dot's Café.

The Essence of Saffron in Scripture

The Patient Harvest

*Crocus sativus – Spice is dried from the freshly
picked stigmas of the flower – native to Iran*

The most costly of all spices in the world, it is mentioned only once in Scripture. Solomon used it in admiration of his bride's patient spirit.

Working the crocus harvest requires patience and endurance. Hand picking enough of the violet crocus flowers (approx. 200,000) to produce a kilo demands fourteen hours of tedious and back breaking labor. The "red gold" – the three stigmas of the flower – yield the spice. Separating them from the flower necessitates additional handwork. To the crocus farmer, the kilo (2.2 pounds) of high quality saffron is worth approximately $10,000.[1] A reputable online herb source retails 0.375 grams for $8.00. Based on available estimates, that may be about ten strands or ½ teaspoon.

Spices make life interesting. Accepting Jesus' priceless gift makes life eternal. He patiently endured ridicule, scorn, mockery, merciless beatings, and crucifixion to open the gates of heaven to believers. He patiently endures our foolishness and sin. He waits with open arms for our return, ready with forgiveness for the first time or the millionth. He eagerly, but patiently, longs to share the final victory – The Marriage Supper of the Lamb – with each one who believes Him for this priceless treasure. Will a dish or two at that feast feature saffron?

Solomon proclaimed his bride's unmatched value, acknowledging the saffron adorning her branches. What decisions required her patient evaluation? What trials begged patient endurance? How many challenges were required for her to cultivate patience in her life?

Consider it all joy, my brethren, when you encounter various trials, knowing that the testing of your faith produces endurance. And let endurance have its perfect result, so that you may be perfect and complete, lacking in nothing.

(James 1:2-8, NASB)

His mom's prayer was for a woman who learns from experience, cultivating patience and endurance to make wise choices. Bathsheba's words encouraged him to look for the woman wise enough to think before she acts.

She evaluates a field and buys it;
she plants a vineyard with her earnings.
(Proverbs 31:16)

Owing to its cost, cheap imitations are often passed off for saffron. Patience is the often dreaded "P" word we would rather avoid. It's not fun walking through trials and delays. Because the cost of patience often soars way above the personal investment we've budgeted, we can be posers too. Making impulsive choices for quicker gain sacrifices our integrity. Faking it, hiding our heads in the sand pretending all is well, ignoring the proverbial elephant in the room, running from God, becoming angry with Him, or blaming someone else all ante up an easier solution, but tarnishes our name. For the Christ follower, it tarnishes His.

What trials and decisions are requiring patience in your life? Armed with a fresh perspective on patience, embrace those situations and persevere, collecting the costly strands of saffron.

Patient endurance teaches us lessons helpful to our next crisis and are of unparalleled worth in helping a friend who stares that challenge in the face tomorrow. The apostle Paul prayed for us to be strengthened with power for the task:

We are asking that you may be filled with the knowledge of His will in all wisdom and spiritual understanding, so that you may walk worthy of the Lord, fully pleasing to Him, bearing fruit in every good work and growing in the knowledge of God. May you be strengthened with all power, according to His glorious might, for all endurance and patience, with joy giving thanks to the Father, who has enabled you to share in the saints' inheritance in the light. He has rescued us from the domain of darkness and transferred us into the kingdom of the Son He loves. We have redemption, the forgiveness of sins, in Him.
(Colossians 1:9-14)

[1] Grant, Amy, "Saffron Harvest Info: How and When to Pick Saffron," February 22, 2016, *Gardening Know How, http://www.gardeningknowhow.com/edible/herbs/saffron/saffron-harvesting-information.htm*

A Woman of the Bible Displays the Fruit

Unexpected Rewards

Quite honestly, most people are quick to "write someone off." But our God is a God of the second chance. Learn from One who is patient with you, and you'll learn to be patient with others. [1]

~~Woodrow Kroll

The fruitful land sat at the crossroads of the ancient Spice Route and Incense Trail. With famine in Judah, Naomi and Elimelech relocated and raised their family in this foreign land. Their two sons took wives from the Moabite people and enjoyed life together.

Enjoying life included food. Living in close proximity to the ancient trade routes provided ready access to exotic spices of the Near East and the Far East. Their spice purchases most likely included high dollar saffron. Inquiring of the steep price tag, they learned of the painstakingly slow work in plucking those saffron pistils and allowing them to dry before the "red gold" was sent on to colorful markets along the route. Ruth and Naomi likely brought some along on their trip to Bethlehem.

When her husband and her sons died, Naomi received word the famine ended, and she chose to return home. Both daughters-in-law began the journey with her. After serious discussion, the younger women chose differently. Orpah returned to her family and friends in the pagan land of Moab. Ruth chose to follow Naomi and her God.

Do not urge me to leave you or turn back from following you; for where you go, I will go, and where you lodge, I will lodge. Your people shall be my people, and your God, my God.

(Ruth 1:16, NASB)

The women arrived in Bethlehem in the spring, just in time for the barley harvest. Many Mediterranean dishes include saffron.* They delighted they owned a supply.

To remarry, as well as to be provided for, Ruth needed a kinsman redeemer offering her his hand in marriage. Typically the nearest male relative to the deceased husband received the honors. Ruth asked permission to glean the fields of a local farmer. Without knowing whose it was, she asked to glean in the field of Boaz, a close male relative of the family. Boaz and Ruth married, and they became the great-grandparents of King David. Easily overlooked in this familiar story is the patience Ruth showed in waiting for God to bring the man of His choosing into her life. Boaz clearly recognized it.

> *May you be blessed of the LORD, my daughter. You have shown your last kindness to be better than the first by not going after young men, whether poor or rich.*
> (Ruth 3:10, NASB)

Before leaving Moab, Naomi assured Orpah and Ruth that she was too old to remarry and have more children. They would be better to remain in their own land and remarry there. Ruth courageously chose to return with Naomi, knowing her expectations for a family were improbable. Her patience, just like the patience of those participating in the saffron harvest, paid off. Both reaped pure gold.

The Lord does not delay [as though He were unable to act] and is not slow about His promise, as some count slowness, but is [extraordinarily] patient toward you, not wishing for any to perish but for all to come to repentance. But the day of the Lord will come like a thief, and then the heavens will vanish with a [mighty and thunderous] roar, and the [material] elements will be destroyed with intense heat, and the earth and the works that are on it will be burned up.
(2 Peter 3:9-10, AMP)

Widows had very few opportunities at her moment in history, making Ruth's future without a kinsman-redeemer bleak. Ruth loved Naomi and the One True God Naomi served. Ruth patiently moved forward in faith, and received her beautiful earthly reward. God patiently desires for us to have an incredible eternal inheritance. Acknowledging the kinsman-redeemer concept, take a moment to recognize our Redeemer – Jesus Christ – our kinsman and brother. Our refusal of His marriage proposal leaves us with the bleakest leftovers for the future – eternal life apart from Him.

What about patience in your life? Sadly, kicking the idea of patience to the curb in prayer isn't unusual. Praying for patience opens the doors of ample opportunities to show patience and fail at the test. What circumstances have taught you patience? Did the lesson make it easier to patiently await God's provision or His answer the next time you felt pressed beyond your ability to trust for God's best?

Saffron is a source of copper, potassium, calcium, manganese, iron, selenium, zinc, and magnesium.[2] Its aroma may provide a sense of peacefulness. I recently purchased a tiny half gram of potent and colorful saffron. A blog about cooking with saffron for the first time described the taste – "almost like it wasn't there." The writer assured if they had not used it, the difference would be readily noticeable. That made me smile. It was my reaction to the first saffron rice dish I prepared, as well.

[1] Kroll, Woodrow, *Woodrow Kroll Ministries, www.wkministries.com,* quote found at: http://www.christianquotes.info/quotes-by-author/woodrow-kroll-quotes/

[2] "Guide to Herbs and Spices," January 9, 2013, *Think Eat Live, https://thinkeatlive. wordpress.com/2013/01/09/guide-to-herbs-and-spices/*

Saffron Essence Droplets

Her husband has full confidence in her and lacks nothing of value.
(Proverbs 31:11, NIV)

Fun Facts about Saffron

- Many cultures have used the golden color derived from saffron to dye royal garments.[1]
- The dye from saffron was used as a cosmetic by Cleopatra.[2]
- Saffron is often adulterated and still sold for the same high price. In the Middle Ages anyone selling adulterated saffron was buried alive.[3] Adulteration still happens frequently today. The practice is no longer punishable the same way. Now it's BUYER BEWARE!
- Roman bath water was sometimes infused with saffron. If they were drunk, indulgent Romans might sleep on a pillow stuffed with saffron believing it would "cure" their hangover. [4]
- The flowers are picked precisely at dawn. The flowers are not yet open, helping to preserve the aroma of the stigmas.[5]
- Curry powder includes spices such as turmeric, coriander, cumin, chili pepper, and saffron. When saffron is added it's the star of the show. [6]
- Persian love cakes may include saffron as an ingredient, as well as be decorated with saffron, cardamom, rose, and pistachios to give the dessert an exotic flavor. It looks pretty too! [7]

Your turn

– Watch the saffron harvest. [8]

– Purchase saffron (Crocus sativus) bulbs and have fun growing them. You could even harvest the "red gold."

– Saffron is included in so many Middle Eastern, Indian, and Mediterranean dishes. Look up recipes [9] and experiment with the flavor and aroma for yourself.

– Mix a few crushed saffron stigmas into a glass of lemonade.

[1] Geenen, Rachel, "Fun Facts You Didn't Know...," *Saffron Crocus sativus*, part of a larger work featured on The Multiple Organisms website (University of Wisconsin-LaCrosse students enrolled in Organismal Biology), *https://bioweb.uwlax. edu/bio203/s2012/geenen_rach/facts.htm*

[2] Geenen, Rachel, "Fun Facts You Didn't Know...," *Saffron Crocus sativus*, part of a larger work featured on The Multiple Organisms website (University of Wisconsin-LaCrosse students enrolled in Organismal Biology), *https://bioweb.uwlax. edu/bio203/s2012/geenen_rach/facts.htm*

[3] Geenen, Rachel, "Fun Facts You Didn't Know...," *Saffron Crocus sativus*, part of a larger work featured on The Multiple Organisms website (University of Wisconsin-LaCrosse students enrolled in Organismal Biology), *https://bioweb.uwlax. edu/bio203/s2012/geenen_rach/facts.htm*

[4] Geenen, Rachel, "Fun Facts You Didn't Know...," *Saffron Crocus sativus*, part of a larger work featured on The Multiple Organisms website (University of Wisconsin-LaCrosse students enrolled in Organismal Biology), *https://bioweb.uwlax. edu/bio203/s2012/geenen_rach/facts.htm*

[5] Kinson, Fleur, "Petals and Spice," 2010, *where-to-go-in-italy.com, http://www. where-to-go-in-italy.com/abruzzo-saffron.html*

[6] "Curry Blends," *The Spice House, https://www.thespicehouse.com/spices/curry-powder*

[7] Thorisson, Mimi, "Persian Love Cake," May 13, 2012, *Manger, http://mimithorisson.com/2012/05/13/persian-love-cake/*

[8] Discovery UK, "Saffron – How Do They Do It?," November 18, 2013, Posted to YouTube, *https://www.youtube.com/watch?v=Mna7iUIP2fM*

[9] A "saffron" search on this website showed 228 recipes:

http://www.epicurious.com/

Chapter 5

Calamus – Kindness

Cinnamah-Brosia and Friends
Share about Kindness

Diffusing Today: Lemon Myrtle essential oil

Aromatic Influence: This sweet citrusy aroma may help purify the environment.

Daily Delight: Bagels with tomato preserves and cream cheese spread

Musically: *Thank You* (Ray Boltz)

Verse of the Day:

The local people showed us extraordinary kindness,
for they lit a fire and took us all in, since it was raining and cold.
(Acts 28:2)

"Everything in my life is spiraling out of control! C-B, are you listening, because I've got a bunch of junk I need to dump? I need your ears and your wisdom – and I need them NOW!"

Calling on God and my life experiences, I made my way to the gingerbread leather sofa in front of the fireplace. Haley already parked herself at Sophia's Corner, ready for whatever deep insights she believed I possessed. Haley dramatized things often. I wondered how big the clump of junk was today. Did I have any encouragement for her? I shot an arrow prayer upward, and relied on the Holy Spirit once again to give me courage and kindness to provide Haley the listening ear she needed.

The story poured out in sobs. "Dan needs another back surgery. This will make the third. The doctors just can't seem to put him back together right since his fall at work. His disability pay is a lot less than his salary, and it doesn't look like they'll let him come back. I need time off to be with Dan, and somebody needs to be responsible for Jax while he recovers. I've got his doc's letter, but my company isn't interested. It was all the excuse they needed. They let me go today. I'll receive unemployment, but what little it is – how will we ever make it? Dan doesn't know yet, and Jax needs to believe nothing has changed. It feels like God hates us. I'm so sorry I'm such a mess. I came straight here, C-B, because you always have the right words and the best stories to make me believe it will be alright."

"Haley, I completely relate to your story. You may find it a real stretch to believe how similar ours is. When Jeremy and I moved our family back here to help Gram and Jeremy's dad, there was much more to that decision than many knew. That was 2001. The dot-com world had crashed the year before, and the economy went with it. Jeremy had been out of a job for six months. We had three small children. My company had two nurses on staff for their employees and saw fit to cut that down to one. You can guess who was canned. We were already deeply behind on the budgeted necessities and released our grip on one luxury after another. Jeremy never dreamed he would come back to this small town to live, but his dad's company needed to expand and upgrade its computer systems. Jeremy's expertise boosted their ability to do that. Gramps died a few months earlier, and Gram needed help. Our options depleted, we moved back.

"Today, his dad's company is thriving. Gram and I together kept the café doors open (and our guests kept them swinging). Our children grew up in the midst of this wonderful oasis of friends and family. Credit for the renovation ideas all goes to Kaitlyn and Gram. Keeping it vintage with a twist, Cinnamah-Brosia's Coffee Cottage and Gift Shop far exceeded my expectations. Kaitlyn's amazing talent, dedication to her family, and her love for Jesus make this mom's heart burst.

"Thing is, Haley, for a while we threw a pity party, smacked a lot of blame around, and screamed at God. We needed desperately to find courage to trust Him, instead, to provide the best future for our family. It was tough. The enemy doled out chunks of doubt. We experienced deep fears. God's plan eluded us, but we chose to believe and pray. And then we prayed for more faith to believe. We hung on tightly to Jesus' promise:

> *The thief comes only in order to steal and kill and destroy. I came that they may have and enjoy life, and have it in abundance [to the full, till it overflows].*
>
> (John 10:10, AMP)

"The kindness of others supplied our lifeline, and God never let us down. We've accepted that our life is very different. Letting go of vain pleasures was painful. Now we see all the glittery trimmings of the world yielded little of the blessings of being here for family and friends and having time with each other. In the middle of life's ups and downs, Jesus' abundant life rocks!"

"Well, that's a sweet fairy tale come true, C-B. Do you really believe God could turn things around for us? That's laughable. Prospects couldn't be bleaker. Where do I even begin?"

"First pray. Tell Dan. Pray together. Find encouragement in God's Word. Choose promises that speak to your heart. Plaster them on your mirror, your refrigerator, your doors, anywhere you'll bop into them several times each day.

"Swallow pride. Yep, that's a huge one! Consider your options, and humbly acknowledge open doors. Accept the kindnesses of friends and family. In fact, with Christmas just a month away, I'm asking my Bible study group to provide gifts for Jax. If you can handle spending time with us 'older' folks, would your family join ours for Christmas dinner?"

Haley and Dan accepted our invitation. Their bleak situation was propelled in a new direction. Dan confided in Jeremy, and a mentoring friendship developed. Dan and Haley began attending church and reading their Bible regularly. They discovered this promise of God, spurring them on to participate in many community outreach opportunities.

> *Whoever is kind to the poor lends to the Lord,*
> *and he will reward them for what they have done.*
> (Proverbs 19:17, NIV)

A year later: Family, friends, and church members helped them with the resources they needed. They courageously fought their battle. Dan's back finally healed. Alex and his dad hired him at their company. Haley landed a position with great hours (more time with Dan, Jax, and the little one on the way). Fellow employees in her new company are kind to one another. The journey was tough, but their lives are full and abundant. All glory to God!

Kindness to the Rescue

Botanical Name: Acorus Calamus; fragrant oil found in all parts of the plant, but generally steam-distilled from the roots; common plant to most of the Old World

Picture a crazy maze – one with lots of twists and turns to get from "A" to "B." We will travel through one to rescue Calamus today.

A dictionary app listed 43 synonyms for kindness. Sweetness made the list! One of the more common ingredients in God's recipe for the Holy Anointing Oil (Exodus 30), Calamus goes by several names including sweet cane, sweet grass, and sweet myrtle. Queen Esther's Jewish name, Haddasah, means Myrtle. Myrtle means sweetness. The app also included these definitions: hospitality, patience, thoughtfulness, unselfishness, gentleness, affection, to name just a few. This character profile for Esther impresses. The time she spent in preparation to approach the king, however, required an empowerment beyond her name.

History records King Xerxes' extremes of emotions, outbursts of anger, and unusual actions. Here's one of them. In 480 BC Xerxes punished the sea by having it whipped 300 times. He blamed the storm for wiping out a bridge constructed for his armies. Some sources claim he may have beheaded many of the soldiers, as well, despite neither sea nor man being responsible for a storm. [1]

Esther's coronation as Queen of Persia occurred two years later. She knew another story, too. The story of his previous queen's removal during one of his tirades spread quickly through the land when he sought a new first lady.

Mordecai, a Jewish exile from Jerusalem, adopted his orphaned cousin, Esther, years earlier. He spent his day near the city gate, staying current on all the news. His prompting placed Esther in the beauty pageant for the successor's selection.

Later, at the same city gate he learned of the impending annihilation of the Jewish people. Mordecai urged Esther to request an audience with the King to avert the impending doom. She knew her request for an audience with Xerxes significantly boosted her chance of punishment (possibly death), if he refused her. Mordecai encouraged Esther to see beyond her fear and vulnerability.

> Mordecai told the messenger to reply to Esther, "Don't think that you will escape the fate of all the Jews because you are in the king's palace. If you keep silent at this time, liberation and deliverance will come to the Jewish people from another place, but you and your father's house will be destroyed. Who knows, perhaps you have come to your royal position for such a time as this."
> (Esther 4:13-14)

Esther and her maids committed to three days of prayer and fasting. She requested and expected the same of Mordecai and the other Jews.

> "Go and assemble all the Jews who can be found in Susa and fast for me. Don't eat or drink for three days, day or night. I and my female servants will also fast in the same way. After that, I will go to the king even if it is against the law. If I perish, I perish." So Mordecai went and did everything Esther had ordered him.
> (Esther 4:15-17)

No amount of kindness, sweetness, hospitality, thoughtfulness, and affection yielded the antidote demanded to soften Xerxes' heart, even in response to his beautiful queen. Prayer and fasting summoned the breakthrough. God answered Esther, her maids, and the Jewish people with divine empowerment that comes only from Him.  The hot-headed royal received her kindness, hospitality, patience, thoughtfulness, unselfishness, gentleness, and affection in a way none of them dared to hope or even imagine. Xerxes reversed the edict and bestowed high kingdom honors upon Mordecai for allegiance and protection of the king.

Myrtle made Solomon's locked garden list. In his Proverbs, he shared this wisdom:

A soft and gentle and thoughtful answer turns away wrath,
But harsh and painful and careless words stir up anger.
(Proverbs 15:1, AMP)

We witnessed kindness in Esther's life. Kindness with commitment to prayer and fasting brought God's response – a resounding "Yes!" With Xerxes' anticipated actions thwarted, the story came to a beautiful conclusion. Myrtle's aroma may bring calm to an inflamed environment. Showing kindness to others offers similar benefits. That comes easily in the good times. Though desperately needed in the more challenging ones, choosing kindness often proves difficult. An action of kindness in those moments may require prayer and fasting.

Esther may be your favorite Bible character, you may know nothing of her at all, or your knowledge of her story is somewhere between those extremes. It's always good to read a new (to you) story or refresh your memories of one you've known forever. Make some time to read Esther. As you do, consider what opportunities you have had to act with kindness toward someone else or on another's behalf when you knew it might not be well received? What was the outcome? How might Esther's story be an encouragement to you to further cultivate this fruit of the Spirit in your life and act with even greater kindness?

Do not let kindness and truth leave you;
Bind them around your neck,
Write them on the tablet of your heart.
(Proverbs 3:3, NASB)

[1] Brians, Paul, et al., editors, "Herodotus: The Histories: Xerxes at the Hellespont (mid 5th Century BCE)," December 18, 1998, from *Reading About the World, Volume I*, 3rd edition, Harcourt Brace College Publishing: ISBN 0-°©-15-°©-567425-°©-0 Pullman Washington, *Washington State University*, http://public.wsu.edu/~brians/world_civ/worldcivreader/world_civ_reader_1/herodotus.html.

A Woman of the Bible Displays the Fruit

Saying Yes to Kindness

"No act of kindness, no matter how small, is ever wasted."
~~Aesop

The question made for a surreal moment. The lady, a stranger to me, shared, "I've sold everything I own, and I'm going to Rwanda. I'll be staying with a pastor and his family there. They have four little girls aged two, four, six, and eight. God clearly told me I would take a dress to each of the girls, and some would come from someone I do not know. This person would know nothing of my plans. Do you think maybe these dresses are the ones?"

My own story began a few months earlier, before I met this woman. I had read about Dorcas' in Acts 9 countless times before, but this time was different. Here's the scoop that caught my attention.

The widows and single moms in the seaport town of Joppa may have been low on cash, but they knew the lady who would meet their fashion needs. Girls learn skills with a needle sitting at the feet of their moms and grandmas. These are great teaching moments for life. Influential women in Dorcas' life instilled a love of God and kindness of heart, training her to share with those less fortunate.

A disciple of Jesus Christ, Dorcas continuously spread kindness and charity using her gift to create tunics and garments for needy ones in her town. When she became sick and died, her friends displayed amazing love for her. The widows carefully cared for her body according to their customs (that included anointing with fragrant oils). They immediately sent for Peter.

They introduced Peter to the sweet myrtle of kindness in the garden of Dorcas' heart. Moved by their tribute, Peter prayed. God raised Dorcas back to life and to them. The level of love, honor, and respect for her in the community is evident in the speed with which the news spread. Many believed in Jesus because of her story. Read it in Acts 9:36-43.

This particular time I read the account, God spoke to me as clear as I have ever heard. "Make two little girls dresses just like Dorcas did." Sizes? Maybe a 2, or a 4, or a 6. I settled on the sizes 2 and 4. God showed me a virtual snapshot of the dresses, too. While sewing projects are quite a normal part of my world, when I began this project, my family was convinced I was crazy. We knew no one who could wear them. What a ridiculous effort and waste of time and resources, right? Feeling a bit unsure of all this myself, but knowing I heard God ask, I made them anyway.

Along with an invitation to a women's ministry Christmas party came instructions to bring a Christmas gift for Jesus. I knew immediately the dresses were the gift. This was not my church home at the time. The woman traveling to Rawanda also attended as a guest. Only He could bring our stories together in such an amazing way. I'm not certain how I responded to her question, but I know it was in the affirmative. A room full of women experienced God's anointed presence, and those dresses were on their way to bless two little girls across the sea.

Calamus showed Solomon's bride possessed a kind heart. Acts 9:36 describes Dorcas as "a disciple...abounding with deeds of kindness and charity, which she continually did." Our Proverbs 31 Lady sewed her clothing and that of her household. Her skill set included sewing. It was in Dorcas' skill set. Sewing is in my skill set, too.

Thankfully, we are all gifted quite differently. God intended it that way. While you may feel like you are all thumbs with a needle, you may be a wonderful cook or a great listener. Organization or motivation may come easily to you. Whatever your gifts, use them confidently to serve in the church and in your community, to provide for your own household, to create gifts for others, or even to establish an entrepreneurial venture – anywhere your kindness may be felt by others.

For we are God's handiwork, created in Christ Jesus
to do good works,
which God prepared in advance for us to do.
(Ephesians 2:10, NIV)

As well as representing sweetness and kindness, calamus' aroma may be supportive of mental refreshing, clear thinking, and discernment. Regularly studying God's word amplifies our ability to clearly discern His voice. When God asks you to use your gift(s) for a specific purpose, He's got the big picture. When you know His voice, you quickly respond, and are privileged to be the hands, feet or mouth of Jesus. Others receive blessings through your kindness.

Was there a specific time in your life when God gave you a vision or direction to use your gift(s) in a very specific way with no explanation on His part? How did you respond? Did you recognize the God moment? (I'm sure many have slipped away, because I was too busy or too disengaged to notice.) What unexpected blessings for you and others resulted from your kindness when you did say, "yes" to the Lord?

Calamus Essence Droplets

When she speaks she has something worthwhile to say,
and she always says it kindly.
(Proverbs 31:26, MSG)

Fun Facts about Calamus

- Calamus was used to make powdered wigs.[1]
- Calamus likes "wet feet," and often grows among cattails, irises, and other water weeds.[2]
- It is not exactly the same plant as Biblical calamus, but calamus is also commonly known as sweet grass.[3]
- Wildlife thrives where sweet grass grows. Mandrakes are especially fond of eating the rhizomes or roots. The seeds provide food for wood ducks. [4]
- Calamus was an ingredient in the original formula for Dr. Pepper®. [5]

Your Turn

– Planting calamus will add a pleasantly sweet citrus (tangerine) scent to your garden.

– Sweet grass grows well in South Carolina, where you will find a vast array of beautifully designed and crafted sweet grass baskets. A most labor-intensive process, your purchase of one of these baskets would be an act of kindness toward the artisan and a reminder of the Holy Spirit's fruit of kindness in your life.

– Experiment: Crush sweet grass leaves, place in an open container, and set it near you when outside. If the ancients are correct, you may easily and successfully deter pesky critters.

– Dorcas sewed dresses for those in need in her community. Make pillow case dresses for *Little Dresses for Africa*.[6] You'll be sending hope and kindness to little girls in need.

[1] "What Is Calamus," *The Epicentre, http://theepicentre.com/spice/calamus-sweet-flag/*

[2] McDonald, Jim, sweetflag/bitterroot, *Jim McDonald "Herbalist," http://www.herbcraft.org/calamus.html*

[3] "Calamus (Acorus calamus) – Calamus Information," *http://www.a1b2c3.com/drugs/var002.htm*

[4] "Plant Fact Sheet: Sweet Flag Acorus calamus L. Plant Symbol = ACCA4," USDA NRCS *United States Department of Agriculture Natural Resources Conservation Service, Rose Lake Plant Materials Center, https://plants.usda.gov/factsheet/pdf/fs_acca4.pdf*

[5] Turiano, John Bruno, "Spice Rack: Calamus," February 6, 2015, *Westchester, http://www.westchestermagazine.com/Westchester-Magazine/February-2015/What-Is-Calamus/*

[6] "We're Not Just Sending Dresses, We're Sending Hope," *Little Dresses for Africa, www.LittleDressesforAfrica.org*

Chapter 6

Cinnamon - Goodness

Cinnamah-Brosia and Friends
Share about Goodness

Diffusing Today: Cinnamon and Juniper essential oils

Aromatic Influence: Warm and inviting sweet cinnamon with evergreen aromas, may help fill the environment with feelings of abundance and a sense of peacefulness

Daily Delight: Cinnamon Rolls, of course!

Musically: *Do Something* (Matthew West}

Verse of the Day:

Surely goodness and mercy shall follow me all the days of my life: and I will dwell in the house of the Lord forever.
(Psalm 23:6, KJV)

Jiggers can be so devastating. The parasitic sand fleas burrow and lay their eggs inside the feet. Without intervention, the cycle repeats again and again. Disease. Crippling. We had just watched Sole Hope's video on this dilemma in Uganda, and we were cutting up our old jeans. The members of their community believe the jiggers to be a curse or witchcraft. Stigmatized, many do not seek treatment. They live as outcasts.

A few weeks earlier Jane scooped this story from a recent blog post.[1] She was leading our group in a discussion on goodness. Our ladies took a serious look at Bible verses about "goodness." We posted some favorites to our "page."

Mankind, He has told you what is good and what it is the Lord requires of you: to act justly, to love faithfulness, and to walk humbly with your God.
(Micah 6:8)

I know that there is nothing better
for people than to be happy
and to do good while they live.
(Ecclesiastes 3:12, NIV)

Who is wise and understanding among you? Let them show it by their good life, by deeds done in the humility that comes from wisdom.
(James 3:13, NIV)

Always on the lookout for practical ways to help others, Gram's life radiated generosity and kindness. Our group discussion fueled my passionate desire to continue Gram's legacy in intentional ways. "What a perfect activity for a Fish and Beans night at the coffee cottage. Let's plan for the last Saturday of the month. Spread the word we're hosting a shoe cutting party!"

Tonight was the night. Wow! Thirty people showed up with their old jeans and scissors. Frank was present and humming one song after another, the cue he knew a great community interest story when he saw it. Kaitlyn and I had readied the room right after closing. Crystal collected scissors, markers, safety pins, milk jugs, and zipper bags. She arrived early to set up the tracing, cutting, pinning, and bagging stations we would need. We requested the musicians for the evening share songs about serving others. Holt arranged Sophia's Corner for he and his friend.

The cottage was bustling as men, women, and children appeared with their old jeans in hand. There wasn't a dry eye as we began cutting. Moved by the stories we watched and the music we heard, we eagerly prepared materials for sixty pairs of shoes to go to *Sole Hope*.[2] We imagined the faces of those who would earn a wage and learn a skill while sewing them, and of others in the communities participating and serving in support roles. We listened when Jane read beautiful testimonies of healing and hope from the organization's blog. Concluding the evening, we joined hands and prayed over the shoe kits, those who would sew them and help in other ways, and the people whose feet would wear them. The room was impregnated with the weight of the Holy Spirit empowering this goodness for God's glory.

From that point forward, our little group prioritized a monthly Fish and Beans service night. Knowing fully that there were many more opportunities like this one, Crystal committed to choosing our next project. We knew for sure there would be more shoe cutting parties, too. My heart danced!

[1] "Sole Hope Stories & Updates," *Sole Hope*, *http://www.solehope.org/blog/*

[2] Host your own shoe cutting party." The shoe pattern/instructions may be ordered here: **Shoe Cutting Party Packet**, *http://sole-hope.myshopify.com/products/shoe-cutting-party-packet*

The Essence of Cinnamon in Scripture

God's First Recipe for Goodness

Botanic Name: Cinnamomum verum; oil steam-distilled from the bark of the tree; native to China, East India, Ceylon (current day Sri Lanka), Malabar (Southwest coast of India)

Was Solomon's bride a whiz in the kitchen? Had he enjoyed her culinary delights? Did she bake bread with cinnamon goodness tucked inside? Did he inhale the sweet aroma and trust their home would be a place of sanctuary overflowing with goodness and blessings?

You'll regularly find me baking bread for my family from freshly milled grain, setting aside a portion of the dough for cinnamon rolls or cinnamon bread. The cinnamon bread oozes brown sugar, cinnamon, raisins, nuts and occasionally drips that gooey white icing.

Breathing in the aroma as it bakes recalls delicious memories with people we love. Our other senses are far more cautious, but our sense of smell causes us to react spontaneously, transporting us back in time to people, places, and experiences.

One dictionary definition of goodness: *being a beneficial or nourishing element of food.*

Cinnamon's aroma may evoke feelings of abundance. It offers help to support healthy digestion and healthy immune systems. It tastes and smells fabulous and may physically enrich our lives as well.

Moses' ingredients list for both the Holy Anointing Oil and the Holy Incense included cinnamon. The recipe belonged to God; the first one shared with his creation. The priests butchered many animals for the required sacrifices. Cinnamon may have helped ensure their physical well-being, while its fragrance created an aromatic refuge for them. God knows the goodness of cinnamon!

"O taste and see that the Lord is good;
how blessed is the man who takes refuge in Him!"
(Ps 34:8, NASB)

We taste, we see, the Lord is good. His presence is our refuge, too. The bread is not filled with cinnamon, but God gave us a reminder of the goodness of His presence in our lives and a reminder of why He is our refuge when Jesus instituted the Lord's Supper. Jesus, The Bread of Life, poured out His own lifeblood for us. He set aside the bread and wine of the Passover as a remembrance meal for us.

Jesus said to them, "I am the bread of life;
he who comes to Me will not hunger,
and he who believes in Me will never thirst.
(John 6:35, NASB)

Cultivating the fruit of the Spirit in our lives, we reflect the character traits of our prefect Creator. Sinful creatures we are, we are still made in His image. By design, we share in His character. Goodness relates to moral excellence. Solomon recognized and trusted his bride's principled character.

The heart of her husband trusts in her,
and he will not lack anything good.
(Proverbs 31:11)

Cinnamon rolls top the menu favorites at Cinnamah-Brosia's Coffee Cottage and Gift Shop. Her recipe is shared below. My own recipe for cinnamon bread and rolls using the freshly milled grain is found on our website.[1] Jesus and the

Father are preparing a wedding feast for all who believe and trust in Jesus as their personal Lord and Savior. I'm praying cinnamon rolls are on the menu!

When spending time with you, do others taste the safety of God's goodness? Are they free to share their secrets with you, without fear of ridicule or gossip? Is your encouragement morally excellent, pouring from the goodness and truth of His Word?

[1] Watson, Lynn, "Cinnamon Bread Goodness," August 4, 2016, *Lynn U Watson Author, http://lynnuwatson.com/cinnamon-bread-goodness/*

Cinnamah-Brosid's Orangey Cinnamon Rolls

Recipe adapted from King Arthur Flour Recipe

Dough:
1 packet instant yeast
1 cup hot water from tap
3 cups unbleached all-purpose flour
3 Tbsp. butter at room temperature
3 Tbsp. coconut oil at room temperature
3 Tbsp. honey
¼ cup nonfat dry milk
½ cup instant mashed potato flakes

Cinnamon Filling:
¼ cup granulated sugar
1 ½ tsp. ground cinnamon
2 tsps. Unbleached all-purpose flour
2 tsps. Milk, to brush on dough
¼ tsp. nutmeg
Zest from one medium or two small oranges

Orange Vanilla Glaze:
1 ¼ cup confectioners' sugar
½ tsp. vanilla
1 Tbsp. orange juice
Slowly add enough milk to make a soft spreadable icing

Directions:

- Combine the instant yeast with all other ingredients for the dough. Mix together until dough is smooth. A stand mixer is recommended (approximately 7 minutes on setting 2 with dough barely clearing sides of bowl). This step may be done by hand.
- Lightly grease a bowl (cooking spray works well). Place the dough in the bowl and cover with a clean kitchen towel. Let rise until it doubles in size. At room temperature this may take 1-2 hours. Setting it in your oven with the oven light on or the oven set to "bread raising" will speed this process.
- Lightly grease two 9" round cake pans. Cooking spray (with lecithin in the ingredients) works well.
- Lightly grease your work surface. Place the risen dough on the surface and roll it into a 16"x12" rectangle. The dough should be very soft. If you do not have a rolling pin available, pat it out.
- Whisk together the ingredients (except the milk) for the filling.
- Brush your dough rectangle with the milk.
- Cover the rectangle completely by evenly spreading the filling mixture over it.
- Roll the rectangle – start at the long side. Seal up the edges carefully.
- Using a serrated knife or dental floss, slice the "log" into 16 pieces. (If using a knife, run it under hot water and wipe it off between each cut to make the process go more smoothly.)

- Place 8 rolls in each pan.
- Cover the pans once again with the clean kitchen towel. Follow same instructions as above for rising. They should begin to spread out, touching each other, filling in the spaces between them.
- Preheat oven to 375° F.
- Bake about 20 minutes. Rolls should be slightly brown around the edge and beginning to turn a golden brown across the tops.
- Mix together ingredients for the glaze.
- Remove rolls from pan. Spread icing on rolls and ENJOY!!

A Woman of the Bible Who Displays the Fruit

Goodness in the Garden

Of all virtues and dignities of the mind, goodness is the greatest,
being the character of the Deity;
and without it, man is a busy, mischievous, wretched thing.
~~Francis Bacon

Grampa was the impatient kind when it came to his garden. Gramma directed her friendly admonishments, as he and I often picked the fruits of their labor before they were ready. The temptation was too great for both of us. We were eager to taste those radishes, onions, and other veggies we had planted and cultivated for weeks. Thankfully our temptations were not forbidden fruit.

With all the challenges to the integrity of our food supply, backyard gardening has returned with enthusiasm. Whether you live in the city or the country, you may have jumped on this train. The wide array of reality television programming includes a show where people are buying a farm. With limited space, others have located gardens in the front yard or patio of their urban or suburban homes. Some enjoy community gardens with shared bounty or visit local farmers' markets regularly.

Adam and Eve tended a garden like no other and feasted from its goodness. Absolutely the best kitchen garden and flower garden ever, I'm absolutely positive there were cinnamon trees!

Then God said, "Let Us make man in Our image, according to Our likeness. They will rule the fish of the sea, the birds of the sky, the livestock, all the earth, and the creatures that crawl on the earth." So God created man in His own image; He created him in the image of God; He created them male and female. God blessed them, and God said to them, "Be fruitful, multiply, fill the earth, and subdue it. Rule the fish of the sea, the birds of the sky, and every creature that crawls on the earth." God also said, "Look, I have given you every seed-bearing plant on the surface of the entire earth and every tree whose fruit contains seed. This food will be for you, for all the wildlife of the earth, for every bird of the sky, and for every creature that crawls on the earth—everything having the breath of life in it. I have given every green plant for food." And it was so. God saw all that He had made, and it was very good. Evening came and then morning: the sixth day.

(Genesis 1:26-31)

Of all the animals God created, not one of them was right for Adam. God had his created son take a nap, and while he snoozed, God fashioned a woman from Adam's own flesh. Adam fell in love and named her Eve, a name meaning "the mother of all the living." The man and woman were created in God's image and given a superb array of fruits, veggies, and seeds. This was the sixth and final day of creation. God, extremely pleased with all that He had made, declared it to be "very good."

There was one forbidden fruit. And, yes, Eve ate first. Eve, full of goodness and mother of every one of us, made the first gardening blunder.

> *God took the Man and set him down in the Garden of Eden to work the ground and keep it in order. God commanded the Man, "You can eat from any tree in the garden, except from the Tree-of-Knowledge-of-Good-and-Evil. Don't eat from it. The moment you eat from that tree, you're dead."*
> (Genesis 2:15-17, MSG)

We are not told how well Adam communicated God's message. Eve had no idea what a temptation looked like before the serpent came knocking. He was a more beautiful creature then as opposed to the snake that sends most of us screaming and running for a hoe. She listened to this master of deception paint a beautiful picture of sin. He captivated her with a story of desire she couldn't refuse. She turned to Adam, and he ate, too. That mistake defines the hallmark of our thoughts about our first parents in that first garden.

God loves us in spite of our foolish choices. He loved Eve. God chose goodness for His creation. The folly in eating the apple carried consequences, but God's reprimands and punishment included a promise to Eve.

> *Because you've done this, you're cursed, cursed beyond all cattle and wild animals, cursed to slink on your belly and eat dirt all your life. I'm declaring war between you and the Woman, between your offspring and hers. He'll wound your head, you'll wound his heel.*
> (Genesis 3:14-15, MSG)

Our enemy camouflaged himself well and wielded his cunning and manipulative powers in their lives, seducing Adam and Eve to live far from the goodness of the garden. No goodness remained in him, and the serpent lost his stature that day. He became an enemy of God, cursed to crawl on his belly and eat dirt.

Adam and Eve were punished, too, but God offered a promise to this woman He loved. Through her offspring we gain The Savior who defeats Satan forever. This promise assured Eve (and you and me) of the most goodness hoped for in this life. Cinnamon's aroma may attract bounty, but for the Christ-follower, the greatest wealth imaginable springs from the assurance of spending eternity in heaven with Jesus enjoying the incomprehensible goodness He is preparing for us. Feast on the ooey gooey cinnamon rolls from the Holy Spirit garden while awaiting the day we enter the gates of the Holy City to live forever. The Tree of Life awaits us there.

> *Then he showed me a river of the water of life, clear as crystal, coming from the throne of God and of the Lamb, in the middle of its street. On either side of the river was the tree of life, bearing twelve kinds of fruit, yielding its fruit every month; and the leaves of the tree were for the healing of the nations . . . Blessed are those who wash their robes, so that they may have the right to the tree of life, and may enter by the gates into the city.*

(Revelations 22:1-2, 14, NASB)

Cinnamon Essence Droplets

She rewards him with good, not evil, all the days of her life.
(Proverbs 31:12)

Fun Facts about Cinnamon

- Quills of cinnamon (sticks) are made from the dried bark of the tree.[1]
- Cinnamon is in the top five of all spices used in the world.[2]
- Roman Emperor Nero killed his wife. To cover for his remorse, he had cinnamon (a year's supply) burned at her funeral.[3]
- For the Romans, cinnamon was fifteen times more costly than silver.[4]
- Cinnamon is an excellent source of fiber, calcium, and iron. It is also high in fiber.[5]
- In the American home, the most popular seasonings are cinnamon, salt, and chili powder.[6]
- A war between the Dutch and the Portuguese was fought over the island of Ceylon (current day Sri Lanka) in the seventeenth century because of the high demand for the spice. [7] Almost all of the higher quality Ceylon cinnamon still comes from this tiny island off the southeast coast of India.[8]
- Cassia cinnamon is the one most commonly found in the grocery store. Sweeter and higher quality cinnamon is the Ceylon variety. It also commands a higher price.[9]

Your turn:

– Goodness was born in a manger. There are several ideas for a Christmas ornament stable made from cinnamon sticks. Search your favorite DIY social media site and enjoy some fragrant fun.

– Add cinnamon and honey to cream cheese for a great bagel topping.

– Add a little zing to your smoothie by adding cinnamon. Amount varies by your desired taste.

– Cinnamon Scented Pinecones

- Gather pinecones (or purchase at local craft store)

- Set them on a cookie sheet in the oven at 200 degrees for 30-60 mins to ensure no critters left inside.

- Remove from oven and place in zippered bag. Add a few drops of Cinnamon Bark essential oil to the bag. Zip shut. Shake bag. Let sit for several hours or overnight to absorb the aroma.

– Spread Goodness in your community and around the world. A few suggestions; you probably know several more.

- Host a Sole Hope shoe cutting party – Sole Hope, *www.solehope.org*

- Sponsor a Compassion child – *Compassion International, www.compassion.com*

- Pack a box for Operation Christmas Child – *Samaritan's Purse, www.samaritanspurse.org*

- Sew a purse for Sew Powerful – *Sew Powerful, www.sewpowerful.org*

- Provide Christmas gifts for prisoners' children – *Prison Fellowship, www.prisonfellowship.org*

- Ring the bells for your local Salvation Army – *The Salvation Army www.ringbells.org*

NOTE: Of all the many, many wonderful ways to experience the goodness of cinnamon, the "cinnamon challenge" is not one of them. Please do NOT attempt it. [10]

[1] janaka849's channel, "The Cinnamon Story, World's Best Cinnamon, - Ceylon Cinnamon", February 9, 2012, video uploaded to *YouTube, https://youtu.be/4GO-rxNl6M0*

[2] "Top 10 Most Popular in the World of Spices," December 22, 2014, *Odd Stuff Magazine, http://oddstuffmagazine.com/top-10-popular-world-spices.html*

[3] Synan, Mariel, "Cinnamon's Spicy History," October 4, 2013, *Hungry History*™, *http://www.history.com/news/hungry-history/cinnamons-spicy-history*

[4] Kilroy, Jake, "7 Unique Facts That You Didn't Know About Cinnamon," Food News, October 2016, *Foodbeast, http://www.foodbeast.com/news/7-unique-facts-that-you-didnt-know-about-cinnamon/*

[5] "Spices, cinnamon, ground [Cassia] Nutrition Facts & Calories," SELFNutritionData: know what you eat, *http://nutritiondata.self.com/facts/spices-and-herbs/180/2*

[6] "Fun Cinnamon Facts and Recipes," *The Great American Spice Company, http://blog.americanspice.com/index.php/fun-cinnamon-facts-and-recipes/*

[7] "Cinnamon – The Story of a Spice, Wars and Corporations," *ekaloria, http://ekaloria.com/cinnamon-the-story-of-a-spice-wars-and-corporations/*

[8] Synan, Mariel, "Cinnamon's Spicy History," October 4, 2013, *Hungry History*™, *http://www.history.com/news/hungry-history/cinnamons-spicy-history*

[9] "Types of Cinnamon: Ceylon, Cassia, Saigon and Korintje," *Cinnamon Vogue, http://www.cinnamonvogue.com/Types_of_Cinnamon_1.html*

[10] Peckham, Matt, "The 'Cinnamon Challenge' Is a Really, Really Bad Idea: What's the stupidest thing you'd do to score hits on YouTube? Swallow a heaping spoonful of dry cinnamon?," April 23, 2013, *TIME, http://newsfeed.time.com/2013/04/23/the-cinnamon-challenge-is-a-really-really-bad-idea/*

Chapter 7

Frankincense - Faithfulness

Share about Faithfulness

Diffusing Today: Frankincense and lemon essential oils

Aromatic Influence: This combination creates a sweet woodsy pine and lemon aroma that may help provide a refreshing environment of spiritual connectedness.

Daily Delight: Lemon Meringue Pie

Musically: The Cause of Christ (Kari Jobe)

Verse of the Day:

> *Do not those who plot evil go astray?*
> *But those who plan what is good find love and faithfulness.*
> (Proverbs 3:3, NIV)

"Busted!" There I was with my hands in the air dancing around the coffee cottage with a big grin on my face when Jeremy unexpectedly walked through the door. He had seen me giddy with joy many times, but I wondered how long he watched before he announced himself today.

"Oh Jeremy, God and I had such an awesome visit this morning. He showed me something amazing, and He invited me to celebrate!"

"You remember how my friend, Star, had gone through some rough waters awhile back. Her twin brother died in a motorcycle accident, and a few weeks later her mother became ill and passed away. She was beyond devastated. She and I were leading our group of at-risk teen girls through a Bible study on Godly values.

"We planned a Princess Party for the perfect wrap. Star pushed herself to be at each meeting with the girls, but you know the planning decisions for the class and the party landed squarely in my lap. I decided each girl would have a lovely crown to remind her of her royal heritage in Christ Jesus. Star received that reminder, too, when I placed the unanticipated extra on her head.

"Through an impulse purchase a few weeks before the party, I owned a vial of 'Oil of Gladness' anointing oil (olive oil with frankincense and myrrh). It rested quietly in my purse, but not in my mind. I prayed for God to reveal His plan for it. Toward the end of the party we gathered as we always did for worship and prayer. I sensed the Holy Spirit telling me, 'Cinnamah-Brosia, anoint Star with the oil.' She desperately needed an uplifting touch. With her permission I did. The whole room filled with the fragrance. An indescribable peace rose among us as.

"Now imagine this, Jeremy, and stop laughing! Cleaning my closet last week produced a big box of castoffs. A brand new, but never worn top jumped from the collection. It was beautiful, but not my style at all. Stop laughing. Why in the world did I make that purchase? The Holy Spirit whispered in my ear, 'Give it to Star.'

"Maybe I should return it instead, and use the money for something more practical. 'Give it to Star,' I heard the words again. "Another argument and another reminder later, I agreed. 'OK, Lord. You have impressed me with Your love and compassion for her. I love her, too. I'll do it.'

"It was perfectly adorable on her, and she loved it. These three incidents remained totally disconnected in my mind – just little stuff – no big deal, you know. This morning I read this in Isaiah.

The Spirit of the sovereign Lord is on me, because the Lord has anointed me . . . to provide for those who grieve in Zion— to bestow on them a crown of beauty instead of ashes, the oil of joy instead of mourning, and a garment of praise instead of a spirit of despair. They will be called oaks of righteousness, a planting of the Lord for the display of his splendor.

(Isaiah 61:1, 3, NIV)

"Three gifts of God for the grieving heart – my obedience allowed me to provide them for Star. My faithful response in the simple things – a crown, oil of joy, and a garment of praise – brought me blessings I never imagined. I lingered in the chill bumps that morning, awestruck by God's grace and His glory."

His master replied, "Well done, good and faithful servant! You have been faithful with a few things; I will put you in charge of many things. Come and share your master's happiness!"

(Matthew 25:21, NIV)

Jeremy smiled the whole time – laughed a little, too. He grabbed me and spun me around some more, celebrating God's continuous faithfulness in our lives.

The Essence of Frankincense in Scripture

Faithful Frankincense

Botanic Name: Boswellia carterii; oil is steam-distilled from the resin "tears," where cuts were made in the bark of the tree; native to Southwest Arabian peninsula, Ethiopia, and Somalia

God enjoys the incense arising from the prayers of His faithful followers. A glimpse of that is seen in Revelation.

The smoke of the incense, together with the prayers of God's people, went up before God from the angel's hand.
(Revelation 8:4, NIV)

Jesus' disciple, John, recorded that verse in the last book of God's Word. A few thousand years earlier, Moses noted it in the ingredient list for God's very first recipe: Holy Incense. God instructed Moses of

its perpetual/faithful use by Aaron on the Altar of Incense. He further specified Moses' taking holy incense into the tent of meeting where he and God met together. Its aroma may enhance and elevate spiritual connectedness. For Moses, perhaps frankincense' aroma connected him more deeply to the LORD.

"'Aaron shall burn fragrant incense on it; he shall burn it every morning when he trims the lamps. When Aaron trims the lamps at twilight, he shall burn incense. There shall be perpetual incense before the Lord throughout your generations." ... Then the LORD said to Moses, "Take for yourself spices, stacte and onycha and galbanum, spices with pure frankincense . . . and put part of it before the testimony in the tent of meeting where I shall meet with you; it shall be most holy to the LORD."

(Exodus 30:7, 34-36, NASB)

Growing up in a good Jewish home, Solomon, son of King David, learned the significance of the holy incense and the history of Moses and the high priests interceding on behalf of God's people. He witnessed the effectiveness of his parents' continuous and fervent prayer. His father wrote psalms we still pray today. His mother's Godly counsel flowed from time spent acknowledging God's hand and blessings for herself and her family. Solomon's blessing connected frankincense with faithfulness, applauding his bride for bringing a faithful prayer life to their marriage.

Frankincense won its fame from its supporting role in the story of Jesus' birth. Mary, Joseph, and Jesus probably lived in Egypt when the Magi visited. The Egyptians highly prized the costly oil, believing it may help support the wellness of their entire being (body, mind, and spirit). Mary and Joseph knew its special meaning for God's people, because they, too, would have learned from Moses' writings.

Solomon's wealth afforded him easy access to the precious oil. For Jesus and his blue-collar family, the kings presented not only an extravagant gift, but also a very practical one. One tiny drop of essential oil goes far. This gift easily represented a lifetime supply. Jesus' faithfulness, on the other hand, keeps on giving for an eternal lifetime. The wise men knew the traditions of the gifts they laid before baby Jesus, as well. Frankincense acknowledged the ultimate high priestly role He holds.

We have this hope as an anchor for our lives, safe and secure. It enters the inner sanctuary behind the curtain. Jesus has entered there on our behalf as a forerunner, because He has become a high priest forever in the order of Melchizedek.
(Hebrews 6:19-20)

For there is one God and one mediator between God and humanity, Christ Jesus, Himself human, who gave Himself—a ransom for all, a testimony at the proper time.
(1 Timothy 2:5-6)

Mary and Joseph's trust in God possibly flourished from the importance they placed on faithfulness in prayer. Likely, they modeled that to their Son. Jesus devoted time early each morning talking to His Father. Additional conversations continued throughout His day. He knew His Father's voice, and His Father's love. He acted in perfect obedience to His Father. An unwavering commitment to time with Him assures us of knowing the voice of our God and His love for us. Jesus illustrates this beautifully by the example of sheep and their shepherd.

"When he (shepherd) has brought all his own outside, he goes ahead of them. The sheep follow him because they recognize his voice. They will never follow a stranger; instead they will run away from him, because they don't recognize the voice of strangers."
(John 10:4-5)

A few chapters later, Jesus' words brought together the importance of Him as the ultimate mediator between God and man, and placed high value on time we invest in conversation with Him.

"I am the way, the truth, and the life. No one comes to the Father except through Me. If you know Me, you will also know My Father. From now on you do know Him and have seen Him."
(John 14:6-7)

Harvesting frankincense means collecting the tears. The bark of the tree is cut, and resin is allowed to weep from the slits. Pain and challenges often drive us to our knees in tear soaked prayers. David cried out to God that his bed was soaked with tears because of his enemies.

I am weary from my groaning;
with my tears I dampen my pillow and drench my bed
every night.
(Psalm 6:6)

Jesus shed tears in prayer. In fact, at one point His sweat dropped to the ground as tears of blood.

He prayed more fervently, and he was in such agony of spirit that his sweat fell to the ground like great drops of blood.
(Luke 22:44, NLT)

While this occurred, Jesus' disciples, who had been asked to keep watch with Him, dozed.

Jesus invited Peter, James, and John to come with Him. Jesus went to a spot just beyond them. Three times He came back to these sleepy heads. He called out to Peter, but spoke to all of them and to us:

Then He came to the disciples and found them sleeping. He asked Peter, "So, couldn't you stay awake with Me one hour? Stay awake and pray, so that you won't enter into temptation. The spirit is willing, but the flesh is weak.
(Matthew 26:40-41)

"Doing what is right" requires faithfulness in prayer. We easily allow the stuff of life to get in the way of our quiet time for a day or two. We forget our appointment again and again. We lose our faithfulness to the One who desires our friendship and sees us through all our junk, guiding us to do what is right. He longs to spend time with us and to love on us. He's the very best friend we'll ever have. He extends a privileged invitation to hang out with Him any time, any place, and every day, until we meet Him face to face. He inhales the frankincense of our prayers and joins in our excitement and joys. He sympathizes with our tears.

Do you have a friend who holds you accountable in your walk with Jesus? Do you do the same for them? How awesome if you do. If not, would you pray for God to bring that person into your life? He faithfully provides good things for His children.

 Note: Frankincense and incense are mentioned fifty-two times in Scripture. In translation from Hebrew and Greek, whenever it is mentioned as incense, it at least includes some measure of frankincense as in the Holy Incense above.

A Woman of the Bible Displays the Fruit

She Never Left His Presence

Ordinary faithfulness leads to extraordinary impact.[1]
~~Matthew Barnett

Scripture tells us of many faithful women, but today we're awarding the gold medal to Anna!

> *And there was a prophetess, Anna the daughter of Phanuel, of the tribe of Asher. She was advanced in years, having lived with a husband seven years after her marriage, and then as a widow to the age of eighty-four. And she never left the temple, serving night and day with fastings and prayers.*
> (Luke 2:36-37, NASB)

According to the custom, Jesus' parents presented their infant Son to the Lord at the temple. A righteous man named Simeon, filled with the Holy Spirit, recognized the tiny infant as the Lord's Christ. God promised him his eyes would not close in death until he saw the Savior of the world. Simeon spoke blessings over Jesus and His family. And who also faithfully served and prayed in the temple that day but Anna, of course! Frankincense carpeted her prayer life, because the incense burned in the temple day and night. The continuous aroma of this grounding essential oil heightened her prayer life.

Anna married as a young woman. She was widowed seven years later. From that day on, she made the temple her residence. She served and prayed night and day. Anna celebrated 84 birthdays when the Baby visited the temple with His family.

Few opportunities presented themselves for a widow at that time. Was her kinsman-redeemer identified? Did he shirk this responsibility? What part had her family played in her choice? Was her family alive? Had God asked her to serve Him this way? Had her friends laughed at the absurdity of her decision? How much courage do you believe her commitment required?

Anna spent all her time in the temple. With Jesus' death and resurrection, for those of us living A.D. our bodies are the temple. His invitation remains a constant, to sit and talk with Him without ever leaving home.

Never let loyalty and faithfulness leave you.
Tie them around your neck; write them on the tablet of your heart.
(Proverbs 3:3)

We are privileged to worship freely. From helping in the nursery, teaching Sunday school, participating in mission outreach, serving in leadership, to passing the offering plate, opportunities to serve in our churches abound. We attend church to visit our friends. All of these are good things. I recently heard a question posed something like this: You go to church for so many reasons, but do you go to church just to be with Jesus – to be in His presence – to meet with Him there?

We live in this crazy politically correct culture where standing for Truth is often a laughable matter. We may go to church for many of those reasons above, but time spent in His Presence in worship, praise, and awe bolster courage to boldly stand for the Truth when we leave His Sanctuary and live in the world. That's where the real difference is seen, and lives are changed for Him and because of Him.

We honor her memory with a gold medal of faithfulness. She was, however, rewarded in a much bigger way. She encountered Jesus! And Scripture tells us her life had quite an impact for the Kingdom.

At that very moment, she came up and began to thank God and to speak about Him to all who were looking forward to the redemption of Jerusalem.

(Luke 2:38)

[1] Barnett, Matthew, Co-Founder of the Dream Center, *www.dreamcenter.org*, quote found at: *AZ Quotes,*

http://www.azquotes.com/author/38018-Matthew_Barnett

Frankincense Essence Droplets

Honor her for all that her hands have done,
and let her works bring her praise at the city gate.
(Proverbs 31:31, NIV)

Fun Facts about Frankincense

- Roman Emperor Nero burned so much frankincense that eventually it required 3,000 camels to carry the amount he requested each time.[1]

- In Alexander the Great's quest to conquer the whole world, he made plans to invade Arabia to control their roads (Incense Trail, Spice Route, and Silk Road) by levying heavy taxes on the caravans. He died before he accomplished this goal.[2]

- Sealed flasks containing frankincense were found in King Tut's tomb when it was opened in 1922. After sitting for 3,000 years, the oil's aroma was as potent as if it had just been distilled today.[3]

- Frankincense has a fresh fruity pine-lemon aroma, making it delicately sweet with woodsy under notes.[4]

- In ancient Egypt, frankincense was placed in wheat silos as a fumigant for the wheat moths.[5]

- Frankincense trees tolerate and thrive in some most unfavorable conditions. They may even grow out of solid rock. The hardier trees produce the best frankincense.[6]

- The very distinctive black eyeliner, kohl, used by Egyptian women is made from grinding up the charred resin from burning frankincense.[7]

Your Turn

– Watch a video showing the frankincense tears being harvested.[8]

– Does your faithfulness have the aroma of frankincense like Anna's did? Consider diffusing frankincense during your own quiet time.

– Create a Stress Chaser Blend of Essential Oils for diffusing; or dilute them 50:50 with coconut oil for a roll-on application; either way inhaling the aroma may bring a sense of calm to the environment.

> 3 drops Orange essential oil
> 3 drops Frankincense essential oil
> 3 drops Cedar wood essential oil

– DIY play dough with frankincense – May help you collect your thoughts or seek purpose while you indulge in some playful fun, inhaling the empowering aroma the whole time.

> 1 cup flour
> 1 Tbsp. vegetable oil
> 1/2 cup salt
> 1 cup water
> 2 Tbsp. cream of tartar
> Food coloring
> Essential oils

- Mix together the flour, salt, cream of tartar, oil, and water in a medium saucepan. Stir in the food coloring and cook on medium-low heat until the dough starts to harden and come together.
- Set on wax paper and allow to cool for a bit.
- To add the oils, roll the play dough into a ball and make a well in the center. Add 5-10 drops of essential oils and knead it into the play dough to spread it throughout the ball. You may prefer other oils. Experiment.
- Store in an airtight container until ready to play.

– <u>DIY Eye Cream Recipe</u>

      3 drops lavender essential oil

      3 drops frankincense essential oil

      1 ounce coconut oil

- Mix well
- Store in small jar
- Apply morning and evening
- Take care to avoid contact with eyes.

[1] "Frankincense Essential Oil Interesting Facts," *Sally's Organics®*, *http://sallysorganics.com/frankincense-2/frankincense-interesting-facts/*

[2] "Frankincense Essential Oil Interesting Facts," *Sally's Organics®*, *http://sallysorganics.com/frankincense-2/frankincense-interesting-facts/*

[3] "Frankincense Essential Oil Interesting Facts," *Sally's Organics®*, *http://sallysorganics.com/frankincense-2/frankincense-interesting-facts/*

[4] Steinbrinck, "Frankincense and Myrrh Health Facts," December 24, 2013, *Natural healthy concepts*, *http://blog.naturalhealthyconcepts.com/2013/12/24/facts-frankincense-myrrh/*

[5] "Frankincense/Olibanum," *2008, Scents of Earth, http://www.scents-of-earth.com/frankincense1.html*

[6] "Frankincense: boswellia carteri," *herbs2000.com, http://www.herbs2000.com/herbs/herbs_frankincense.htm*

[7] Annamarie Skin Care, "7 things You Didn't Know About Frankincense Essential Oil," *annmarie, http://www.annmariegianni.com/7-things-you-didnt-know-about-frankincense-essential-oil/*

[8] "Young Living Essential Oils – Official, Frankincense: Harvesting," September 8, 2010, video uploaded to *YouTube, https://www.youtube.com/watch?v=1ed5hyCsnJM*

Chapter 8

Myrrh - Gentleness

Cinnamah-Brosia and Friends

Share about Gentleness

Diffusing Today: Myrrh and sandalwood essential oils

Aromatic Influence: This combination of oils suggests aromas of warm creamy cedar, vanilla, and sweet earthy black licorice. Together they may help to provide a sense of gentleness and calm in the environment.

Daily Delight: Apple Cake with Brown Sugar Icing

Musically: Something Beautiful (Steven Curtis Chapman)

Verse of the Day:

Always be humble and gentle. Be patient with each other, making allowance for each other's faults because of your love.
(Ephesians 4:2, NLT)

Our family thrived on rudeness and disrespect. We feared being touched. That was reserved for a licking from Dad or a dispute between siblings. You may remember, I shared with Sara how Mom drove that hippie mobile of hers in and out of our lives – a lot! Sometimes she came alone and sometimes she had a ragtag group of friends along. Some of the men were friendly with me in ways I disliked very much. I bottled my pain.

I was born when Mom was just seventeen. She and Dad did marry and had two more children. He assumed all the responsibilities for my two younger siblings and me. He mostly flew solo with the duties of a job, a home, and a family. He expected maturity from us, unrealistic for our age. Our responses often defied his authority, and garnered more rough treatment and inappropriate 'punishments.' Somehow he and mom wrestled through the turmoil. My spirit ached and ached.

Gram was different. I always loved to visit my grandparents and help in the cafe. I felt loved and cherished by both of them. Gram's conversations brimmed full with gentle and kind words. She cared for everyone who needed her. Experiencing Gram's friendly approach helping others inspired my choice to attend nursing school.

While working with patients as a student nurse, I encountered the biggest surprise of my short eighteen years on the planet. Being kind and gentle with patients meant I had to touch those patients! This was a most unexpected challenge. I was so grateful for Gram's example in the summers, but the rest of the year – well, nothing glittered there.

Because of Gram, I came to know Jesus. While attending nursing school I anchored my lifeline to dependence on God and was grateful the dorms were close to Gram's home. In the beginning when I touched my patients, panic and fear reared their ugly heads. I ended many days even more stressed than my patients, resulting in an unhealthy outcome for them and for me.

I walked in to the cafe one day, tears gushing down my cheeks. "Gram, how do I do this? How do you do it? How do you gracefully handle each situation? You maintain control, but you do it with such gentleness. I need some of that. You and Gramps are the only family members who ever hugged me or touched me tenderly. You know just when someone needs a pat on the back, an arm around their shoulder, or a great big Gram hug. You know how my life has been, and I'm not even sure it's okay to touch others."

She opened her Bible with its well-worn cover and pages. "Cinnamah-Brosia, think of this verse whenever you're serving your patients – or anyone else.

All of you, take up My yoke and learn from Me, because
I am gentle and humble in heart, and you will find rest
for yourselves.
(Matthew 11:29)

"When you're gentle with your words, or when you reach out with a gentle touch, you will fill your soul with peace. The ones around you – your family, your friends, your patients – will feel it, too. It's how Jesus did it.

"When his mom encouraged Solomon to find a good wife, she prayed her daughter-in-law would be kind and gentle – meeting the needs of her family and her household even when it wasn't convenient – like the middle of the night – and gently, without complaint. Solomon shared about this very thing in the Proverbs, too.

A gentle answer turns away wrath,
but a harsh word stirs up anger.
(Proverbs 15:1, NIV)

"Ultimately, our gentle answer yields opportunity to share the source of our gentleness," Gram added.

This happened more than twenty-five years ago. I took Gram's advice. One patient at a time, I learned to be gracious with my words and to reach out and touch my patients. I did have opportunities to share the source of my inner peace.

My reminiscing ended when Crystal came in the cafe with her young daughter. Three-year-old Josie was being so careful, but she spilled her chocolate milk. Watching Crystal lose control, reminded me why I keep all those old memories stashed away. Thankfully, the lessons I learned transformed my life. Walking over to the table with some paper towels, I gently soaked up the drink, but not before wrapping my arms around little Josie and offering the hug she so desperately needed right now – the hug I so desperately needed so many times in my childhood.

Crystal's overreaction settled. Both of them cried. Well, Josie's tears almost stopped now except for a few lingering sobs. Josie lost a little confidence that day, and perhaps felt a little like a failure. Crystal had a memory, too. "I remember mom and me coming here so often. I spilled my drink one day just like Josie did. Mom gave me a huge lecture. A few moments later Miss Dot cleaned up the mess and comforted me like you did Josie."

"Gram was like that. She and Gramps modeled the only real Jesus in shoes I knew. I miss them both so much." While embarrassed for her own temper, Crystal listened while I shared Gram's wisdom. It had made such a difference for my life, not only with my patients, but with my husband and children, too. Acknowledging that I'm still far from doing this perfectly every time, I know that through the power of the Holy Spirit that lives in me, I can look a little more like Jesus each day.

The Essence of Myrrh in Scripture

Soothing Touch of Myrrh's Aroma

Botanical Name: Commiphora myrrha;
oil steam-distilled from gum resin;
native to the Southwest Arabian Peninsula and Ethiopia

The aroma of His mother's gentle touch comforted Jesus while He hung on the cross. You did read that correctly. Owing to our unique olfactory system,[1] He reacted before His brain even comprehended the transport in time to memories of His mother's arms. The soldiers offered Jesus wine and myrrh, but He refused it. All He needed to soothe Him at that moment resided in the aroma of the myrrh. Gifted by the kings in recognition of prophecies of His harsh death, it also brought comfort in that hour.

Esther was given oil of myrrh for the first six months of her beauty treatments. (Esther 2:12) Mary was well acquainted with Esther's story. I believe she chose some of the myrrh for her own personal care. Thoughts of Mary caressing Baby Jesus impress us with a snapshot of gentleness. His mother's gentle touch soothed Him many times in infancy and childhood. Myrrh has great staying power and is often used in perfumes as a fixative so the scent will linger.[2] The lingering of the aroma enhanced the experience.

When the Lord is near, we bask in His gentleness with us. We enjoy a delightful sanctuary, as though the aroma of the myrrh were still lingering long after His death and resurrection.

Let your gentleness be evident to all.
The Lord is near.
(Philippians 4:5, NIV)

Solomon complimented his bride's gentle spirit. With gentleness in our garden, our delight and joy in God shines through. The myrrh-like aroma travels still farther as gentleness turns away drama.

Are your words gentle and kind? Do others leave your presence feeling refreshed, myrrh's sweet gentle scent traveling with them and wafting to others in their circles? Words pack a powerful punch. Cultivate yours carefully. Invite the Holy Spirit to do His gardening of your tongue. Start a wave of gentleness. Watch it go viral.

A word out of your mouth may seem of no account,
but it can accomplish nearly anything—or destroy it!
(James 3:5, MSG)

Myrrh was one of the most highly prized oils. In ancient times it often brought twice the price of frankincense, a costly commodity itself. The rich and indulgent of the ancient world purchased an abundance of myrrh. Demand drives price, and the price went higher and higher. Caravans and royal parades announced their grand arrival with billowing clouds of myrrh. The narrator in the Song of Solomon makes clear that everyone noticed the sweet, pleasant, and uplifting aroma of these ostentatious displays – a blessing for everyone, even the peasants, along the way.

Who is this coming up from the wilderness like a column of
smoke, perfumed with myrrh and incense made from all
the spices of the merchant? Look! It is Solomon's carriage,
escorted by sixty warriors, the noblest of Israel,

(Song of Solomon 3:6-7, NIV)

The gentleness of myrrh suggests softness and tenderness, and its potential benefit for supporting healthy skin may be further enhanced when combined with frankincense. Here's a DIY idea for yourself or a gift for a friend.

Myrrh and Frankincense Skin Cream
1 cup whipped coconut oil
10 drops of myrrh
10 drops of frankincense

- Beat coconut oil until fluffy (approximately 5 minutes). Refrigeration for a short time to begin to solidify the oil before beating may be necessary in warmer months/climates.
- Add in essential oils & beat again until blended
- Store in glass jar (In warmer months/climates you may need to store the cream in the refrigerator.)
- Suggested complimentary essential oils that may be added with the frankincense and myrrh:

> Lavender
> Rose
> Rosewood
> Carrot Seed

[1] Mercola, Dr. Joseph, "Why Smells Can Trigger Strong Memories," August 6, 2015, Mercola.com, *http://articles.mercola.com/sites/articles/archive/2015/08/06/smells-trigger-memories.aspx*

[2] "Fixatives and Their Function in Natural Perfumery," February 26, 2015, *eden botanicals, http://www.edenbotanicals.com/eden-botanicals-blog/fixatives-and-their-function-in-natural-perfumery/*

A Woman of the Bible Who Displays the Fruit

Miriam's Gentle Negotiations

*In the long run, the sharpest weapon of all
is a kind and gentle spirit.* [1]
~~Anne Frank

They named her "Bitter." Before berating her parents for the label, recognize that Miriam along with Mary, Marie, and the countless derivatives of those names are among the most common girls' names in the world. (It's my middle name and the middle name of both of my grandmothers.) Jesus' mother bore the moniker. Many more women named Mary reside on the pages of the New Testament. In ancient times the meaning of your name said much about your character. Does that make you wonder what was happening in all these families' lives that their children weren't named something like Joy or Sweetness instead? The name of the resin we call Myrrh – a gift to Baby Jesus – is the same word.

A family reunion precipitated by a famine in Canaan brought the Israelites to Egypt centuries earlier. They lived well for a period of time. Slavery, however, entrapped them for most of those years. The Egyptians abused the Israelites in their work environment, but fed them well. The Lord provided well for His people in their enslavement and also caused their numbers to increase. Miriam arrived on the scene, first-born child of Amram and Jochebed – both of the House of Levi. Pharaoh was plenty scared of being overthrown by the Hebrew multitudes.

Myrrh and Miriam may mean bitter, but the aroma is sweet. Did Jochebed and Amram hope and dream of their child's name providing a sweet aroma for the family and their people? Did they believe she would grow in leadership skills, gently and courageously opposing the disrespect their people faced on a daily basis? At ten years old, Miriam earned the opportunity to show gentleness.

Like frankincense, the tree is cut to ooze the tears of myrrh.[2] Their aroma is sweet, but the process is one of bitter endurance for the tree. Jesus was pierced and bled and died on a tree to provide the sweet aroma of eternal life.

The hearts of Amram, Jochebed, Miriam, and another son, Aaron, were deeply wounded at the thought of losing their infant son and brother. Jochebed placed the basket in the water. Miriam's actions were necessarily gentle as she hid among the reeds of the Nile and waited. When Pharaoh's daughter found the baby, Miriam met the challenge. She assessed the situation while thinking very quickly on her wet feet. The Egyptian princess loved on Miriam's baby brother. In response to the hopeful sight, Miriam simply asked if the assistance of someone to nurse this baby would be helpful. A pleased adoptive "new mom" readily agreed and offered compensation for the task.

Had the family remained in seclusion, praying they wouldn't be found out, Moses would have surely perished. Had Miriam argued for the baby's life, it's doubtful the negotiations would have been so successful.

The sweetness of this girl named "Bitter" saved Moses' life. His mom became his nurse. The whole family told Moses the stories of God's provision from Father Abraham down through the generations. God saved their people in a bittersweet miracle a few centuries earlier when Joseph's brothers sold him to the caravan merchants traveling to Egypt with their loads of frankincense and myrrh. Realized or not, this proved a major crossroads in the history of the Hebrew people.

God orchestrated the outcome of his parents' choice and his sister's actions. Facing another major crossroads in Israel's history, God chose Moses to lead His children out of Egypt. Older siblings, Aaron and Miriam played major roles in the new family business.

As a mentor to the women, Miriam was well loved, most likely because she maintained a gentle spirit in responding to their adversities. The Hebrew people survived and thrived. The ones who left Egypt didn't enter the Promised Land, but their descendants inherited a grand future. From these people comes the Savior of the world, Jesus. Hear His words:

> *"Come to Me, all of you who are weary and burdened, and I will give you rest. All of you, take up My yoke and learn from Me, because I am gentle and humble in heart, and you will find rest for yourselves. For My yoke is easy and My burden is light."*

(Matthew 11:28-30)

> *The gentle are blessed, for they will inherit the earth.*
> (Matthew 5:5)

Is your legacy one of gentleness even in the bitterest of situations? Paradoxical as it appears, inside or outside the church, gentleness is recognized for its strength and strength's effectiveness by its gentleness.

[1] Frank, Anne, *The Diary of a Young Girl – The Definitive Edition*, (Garden City, New York: Doubleday, 1952)

[2] Crampton, Linda, "Frankincense, Myrrh and Amber: Tree Resin Facts and Uses," June 15, 2016, *Owlcation, https://owlcation.com/stem/Frankincense-Myrrh-Amber-and-Other-Plant-Resins*

Myrrh Essence Droplets

She rises also while it is still night,
and gives food to her household,
and portions to her maidens.
(Proverbs 31:15, NASB)

Fun Facts about Myrrh

- Archeologists have discovered wealthy ancients carried myrrh tears in pouches around their necks to help them smell good.[1]
- Myrrh is considered a fixative in the perfume and cosmetic industry.[2]
- Egyptians, both men and women used it in their cosmetics. [3]
- Myrrh grows in a surprisingly tiny area of the world – current day Yemen on the southwest corner of the Saudi Arabian peninsula and a bit of the horn of Africa.[4]
- It was a first century practice to mix myrrh with wine. It was then given to prisoners for pain relief as they were led to their executions.[5]
- One of the gifts given to the Christ child, myrrh is thought to be prophetic of His death. (Gold represented kingship and frankincense represented His kingly robe).[6]

Your Turn

– Diffuse myrrh with other essential oils:

<u>Refreshing kitchen scent</u>

2 drops of pine essential oil

7 drops of eucalyptus essential oil

1 drop of myrrh essential oil

<u>Winter Blend</u>

3 drops of frankincense essential oil

2 drops of myrrh essential oil

1 drop of cinnamon essential oil

4 drops of white fir essential oil

<u>Relaxing and Grounding Blend</u>

4 drops of myrrh essential oil

3 drops of patchouli essential oil

3 drops of ylang ylang essential oil

– <u>DIY Hand Cream for the Gardner</u>

1/4 cup shea butter

1/8 cup sweet almond oil

1 Tbsp. beeswax

10 drops myrrh essential oil

10 drops cedar wood essential oil

- Melt almond oil, beeswax and shea butter in top of a double boiler, stirring as it melts.
- Remove from heat and let stand for 10-15 minutes.
- Stir in the essential oils and pour into a small glass container.
- Pour into a small glass jar. Allow several hours for it to cool and thicken.

– Create the Perfect Gold, Frankincense, and Myrrh Gift for the Holidays [7]

<u>DIY Myrrh Bath Salts</u>

1/2 cup rock salt or Epsom salts (or a mixture of both)

1/2 cup of kosher salt

1 tsp to 1 Tbsp. of olive oil (to desired consistency)

5 drops of myrrh essential oil

3 drops of lavender essential oil

- Mix salts together
- Add the oils a drop at a time
- Pack in small gift jar

<u>DIY Frankincense Sugar Scrub</u>

3/4 cup raw sugar

1/4 granulated white sugar

Up to 1/4 olive oil or coconut oil

5 drops of frankincense essential oil

2 drops of orange essential oil

- Mix sugars together
- Slowly mix in the olive or coconut oil
- Add the essential oils and mix again
- Use a matching airtight small gift jar

<u>Gold</u>

Place gold wrapped chocolate coins in a small burlap drawstring bag.

<u>To finish</u>

Place all three items in a wooden crate with straw or similar material.

[1] "Myrrh, Gale Encyclopedia of Alternative Medicine," 2005, The Gale Group, *ENCYCLOpedia.com*, *http://www.encyclopedia.com/plants-and-animals/plants/plants/myrrh*

[2] Rose, Jean, "Fixatives and What are They? Aromatherapy/Perfumery," JeanRose.net, *All Natural Beauty, http://allnaturalbeauty.us/jeanne_rose_fixatives.htm*

[3] Illis, Judith, "Beauty Secrets of Ancient Egypt," June 1, 2011, *Tour Egypt, http://www.touregypt.net/egypt-info/magazine-mag06012000-mag4.htm*

[4] Main, Douglas, "What Is Frankincense?" December 24, 2012, *LIVESCIENCE, http://www.livescience.com/25670-what-is-frankincense.html*

[5] "Myrrh," Gale Cengage Learning, 2008, altMD, *www.altmd.com/Articles/Myrrh--Encyclopedia-of-Alternative-Medicine*

[6] Biblical Archaeology Society Staff, "Why Did the Magi Bring Gold, Frankincense and Myrrh?," December 1, 2016, Biblical Archaeology Society-Bringing the Ancient World to Life, *Bible History Daily, http://www.biblicalarchaeology.org/daily/people-cultures-in-the-bible/jesus-historical-jesus/why-did-the-magi-bring-gold-frankincense-and-myrrh/*

[7] Huntley, Amy, "Gifts of the Wisemen: Gold, Frankincense and Myrrh," October 20, 2014, *The Idea Room, http://www.theidearoom.net/2014/10/gifts-wisemen-gold-frankincense-myrrh.html*

Chapter 9

Aloes/Sandalwood
Self-Control

Cinnamah-Brosia and Friends
Share about Self-Control

Diffusing Today: Sandalwood

Aromatic Influence: This sweet, warm, vanilla, and woodsy aroma is traditionally found to be potentially supportive for times of meditation and relaxation.

Daily Delight: Chocolate Lasagna

Musically: *Let There Be Peace on Earth* (Vince Gill)

Verse of the Day:

> *A fool lets it all hang out; a sage quietly mulls it over.*
> (Proverbs 29:11, MSG)

Jesus' laws applied to all, and He was not politically correct. News slings itself at us relentlessly. I usually avoid the TV versions flashing one horrendous scene after another of morality and respect gone terribly astray in an out-of-control world. Jesus, please come and fix it all – NOW! I lingered at the house a little longer this morning. Jeremy, still at home too, had the morning news streaming. I caught too much. A tear or two rolled down my cheek at yet another reminder of our anything goes world. No one, it appeared, cared at all what the Bible said. At this moment I thanked God Gram challenged me to memorize so many of its truths. One kept looping my mind and heart this morning. A quick touch on my phone brought it up in a more modern version:

> *Be serious! Be alert! Your adversary the Devil is prowling around like a roaring lion, looking for anyone he can devour.*
> (1 Peter 5:8)

A scan through my social media page proved the Devil devours. Many did exactly what he or she believed right in his or her own eyes. Little evidence appeared for respect, purity, love, and self-control even in the lives of some Christian friends. Humor and entertainment posts often dishonored God. My dismay increased my gratefulness for reading and knowing the last chapter – God is the ultimate Victor. I wondered if my fellow believers would view, sing, dance, or participate in some of this stuff with Jesus in the room. Truth: He resides everywhere! He observes everything! The answer must be, "yes."

> *You will eat there in the presence of the Lord your God and rejoice with your household in everything you do, because the Lord your God has blessed you. You are not to do as we are doing here today; everyone is doing whatever seems right in his own eyes.*
> (Deuteronomy 12:7-8)

A virtual tap on my shoulder reminded me that Jeremy and I had followed our friends into some questionable circumstances more than once when we were dating. We were believers, but the temptations were great, and occasionally we found ourselves participating in activities on God's disapproval list.

Jeremy and I had known each other our whole lives, and were best of friends – at least in the summers. I confided some of the details of my home life to him. I remain grateful always, Jeremy listened without judgment, and together we promised each other we would wait for marriage. The idea of purity was part of the antiquities collection, and our friends snickered and poked fun at us for our choice.

Marriage handed us a new set of opportunities for self-control. In his message for our wedding, Pastor Gary assured us there would be times we would believe each other to be more of a burden than a blessing. We could choose to thank God for each other in those moments, knowing God is good and His mercy is always present; or we could lose control, hurling painful blows at one another. We aimed for God's way, but we were often guilty of the second option. We prayed together and grew together. We had our moments, we had God, and we forgave quickly.

With the arrival of a family, new opportunities for self-control rained down as our children grew. The lack of self-control in my own childhood overshadowed my challenge of handling our children's disobedience with Godly love and discipline, rather than a venomous attack. Gram and Gramps' loving example only occupied about a fourth of my life, but I thanked God for even that much.

We've managed the difficult conversations in our home. We've taught our children love, respect, purity, and self-control – the beauty of a life dedicated to God. The enemy employs a dazzling array of well-packaged lures of deceit for his unsuspecting prey. He awaits the perfect moments to dangle them right before our eyes. We pray our children avoid his traps. Our younger daughter, Caryn, was caught in one of these dilemmas. I prayed for wisdom, as I grasped the opportunity to reaffirm where I believed she stood.

"Mom, I'm struggling to be obedient to this repetitious voice in my head: 'Talk to Allie. Talk to Allie. Talk to Allie.' Allie is making some very poor choices. She still says Jesus is her Lord and Savior, but something has changed. Her behavior is telling a different story. She's buying the line, 'Everyone's doing it.' It's true, most are. Allie's my best friend. We agreed when we gave our hearts to Jesus when we were ten years old, we would hold each other accountable to always do the right thing – the God thing. What if I talk to her about it, and she doesn't want to be my friend anymore?"

We discussed how real her fears were, and how much Allie needed her to be a true friend. The conversation stirred up so many emotions. We were both soaked in tears when Miss Alice and her daughter, Carol, came by. Miss Alice was one of Gram's dearest friends. She and her husband recently retired and moved to a warmer climate.

"I'm here for a visit with Carol. She's filled me in on the transformation of Dot's Café. I demanded to see for myself. It's fabulous. And I'll take a bowl of that ambrosia. You still make that, right? And, by the way, I'm so glad you're using your name from Gram. She always believed you were full of goodness and your life would bear a lot of fruit. I miss her so much. She became like a mother to me when George and I moved here. Her wisdom guided me through a lot of messes." Miss Alice finally took a breath, and realized something was a bit amiss. She apologized just as profusely.

Carol shook her head as I finally got a word in edgewise. "Oh Miss Alice. I'm so happy you came. Please sit down and have a cup of coffee. I'll get that ambrosia, too. While I do, if you don't mind, would you tell Caryn the story of yours and Mr. George's marriage? I think she really needs to hear it today."

Miss Alice loved to tell stories. The ones that might help someone else were best. "Caryn, years ago Mr. George and I drove our marriage straight into the wall of desperation. We loved each other so much, but we thought we knew everything – including more than our parents taught us from their outdated Bible. We blundered our way through the world's version of love. It was the 1960's era. The world was changing rapidly. Hippies and the beginning of the free love movement arrived. There's really nothing new under the sun since the beginning of time, but the wildest sin packaging in those days looked pretty calm compared to today. That didn't matter. Real life was tough from day to day, and we did whatever we thought we needed to get by. Your Gram reached out with something different.

"At first I refused her kindness. Thankfully, she was wise enough to not force feed me. After 14 years of married mayhem,

George and I split up. We continued to date, though. I finally listened to Dot, and turned my life back to Jesus. I knew for this to work, we needed to do it God's way. Following His Word presented the only solution for our broken mess. George didn't believe that was too cool, but he agreed. Within the year he gave his life to Jesus. We remarried. Our new home life was not without problems, but we regretted not doing it God's way first. Reestablishing trust in all the broken places took courage, time, grace, forgiveness, and self-control. I thank our Heavenly Father every single day that your Great Gram loved me enough to lead me to the Truth."

"Thank you, Miss Alice! What a great story. It was great to see you too. I have to run. Allie's waiting for me."

As Caryn took off, I knew Miss Alice's story was safe, but my mother's heart prayed for extra courage for her and that Allie would thank God for the conversation she and Caryn were about to have.

The Essence of Aloes/Sandalwood in Scripture

No Room for Ego

Botanical Name: Santalum album, native to India and Indonesia, fragrant oil steam-distilled from the heartwood (Note: What the Bible refers to as aloes is not the succulent plant we think of today, but rather refers to the sandalwood tree.)

R.I.P., Jesus. One hundred pounds of aloes and myrrh. That's exactly how much Nicodemus brought to prepare Jesus' body for burial. According to the historian, Josephus, the usual amount of spices for burial was one pound. Sometimes for special people in authority forty pounds of the spice might be used. But a hundred pounds!

For fear of being seen in His presence, Nick, a Pharisee and Jewish ruler, earlier came to Jesus under cover of darkness. Jesus could not do what He did unless God was involved, and Nick had questions. It was with him that night, that Jesus first shared about being born again to see the kingdom of heaven. The conversation included the most beloved Bible verse of all time.

For God so loved the world, that He gave His only begotten Son, that whoever believes in Him shall not perish, but have eternal life."
(John 3:16, NASB)

Nick's humbling act preparing Jesus' body for burial represented zero self-indulgence or egocentricity. The beatings and scourges His body endured severely marred Jesus' identity. Awful smells accompanied decaying flesh.

Joseph of Arimathea owned an unused tomb he wished to give to Jesus' family for His burial. Likely, he purchased it for his own final resting place. As a member of the Council, it took courage to even suggest this to Pilate, the man who had sent Jesus to His death.

Joseph of Arimathea came, a prominent member of the Council, who himself was waiting for the kingdom of God; and he gathered up courage and went in before Pilate, and asked for the body of Jesus.

(Mark 15:43, NASB)

Anyone who has planned a funeral recognizes the value of Joseph's contribution. Aloe and myrrh carried a steep price tag, too. Showing utmost love, respect, and reverence in their sorrow, Joe and Nick offered costly, yet priceless, worship to their King. Both men held honorable positions. Government and religious leaders had just crucified Jesus. They mustered courage to value their Jesus over their reputations.

Finessing the delicate situation required myrrh's gentleness. On the surface, the outpouring of sandalwood oil portrays little about self-control. Sandalwood's aromatic value in helping accept others with an open heart and having less regard for self, says, "It's right on!" Their hearts opened generously for Jesus that day.

Self-control implies selflessness, having within us the empowerment of the Holy Spirit to emerge beyond our fears, willingly making a difference for another. That action requires putting aside our own agendas, our needs, and maybe the stuff we mistakenly believe we deserve. It connects us to each other. Aromas of the essential oils suggest an atmosphere of gentleness and deep calm. The sandalwood may have helped further expand their openness of heart and giving.

Reminder: Pomegranates and aloes – love and self-control – bookend the list. Joy, peace, patience, kindness, goodness, faithfulness, and gentleness stand tall on the spines of the volumes they hold in place. Being genuine with any one of these requires unconditional love. To maintain Godly self-control requires being rooted and growing in all of them.

My buttons are easily pushed, and my need for self-control is most evident when I see what I believe to be incompetence in others. Judgment on my part is my sinful perspective. Spending time with Jesus helps me recognize Satan's threat to my Godly response. He's taught me how to punch the off button more quickly. Do I succeed every time? Sadly, I do not. Thankfully, I may return in repentance again and again, expecting the Holy Spirit to continue digging and pruning to increase the quality of His fruit in my heart.

Jesus unselfishly gave up His life for us. His death provided the most lavish and undeserved gift we ever hope for. His heart is all for us. That the Son of God and Perfect Man was willing to die for you and me with all our shortcomings, faults, and YES – our SIN – is totally amazing! More amazing, the grave did not hold Him! He came out of the grave on the third day quite alive – providing proof positive that no one can out give God. Not before, not then, and not after. Jesus' death and resurrection secured eternity for all who believe. Right now He's preparing an amazing and indescribable eternal home for those who know and love Him.

Jesus' followers, how lavish is your love for Him? In what uber extravagant ways do you show that love? Do you worship with abandon, expressing your ultimate thanksgiving for the Risen Jesus Christ?

This book would be incomplete without inviting you to give your life to Jesus, if you have not already done so. Do you believe He is the Christ, the Son of the Living God? Do you have a relationship with Him? Is He your Lord and Savior? The Gospel has been shared here today. To secure your place in eternity, believe Him, receive Him, and live for Him for the rest of your life. The Holy Spirit provides the courage to do it! Pray like this:

> *Father God in Heaven above, I come to You humbly admitting that I am a sinner in need of your forgiveness. By my own power I am totally unable to come to You or live for You. Thank You so much for sending Your Son, Jesus, to die for me. Thank you for raising Him again from the dead – all of this so that by accepting Him as my Lord and my Savior I'm promised an eternity in heaven. Give me the courage to always walk in relationship with You and Jesus, mindful the Holy Spirit cultivates in me the fruits of the Spirit: love, joy, peace, patience, kindness, goodness, faithfulness, gentleness, and self-control. In the all-powerful name of Jesus, I pray. Amen.*

The biggest blessing we could receive from sharing these devotions with you is you making a decision to follow Jesus. We would love to hear from you. Also, please reach out to Christian friends and/or a local Bible believing church. Share your life-changing decision with them and ask them to help you grow your new faith.

Note: "Jewish tradition prohibits embalming, as the blood is considered a part of the body to be buried with the deceased. Every speck of blood, as well as any hair that comes loose while preparing the body, is gathered in a linen bag and placed in the casket with the body."[1] From Scripture we learn the Jewish people typically wrapped their dead in linen with spices for burial. Historical records indicate these were not ordinarily aloes and myrrh, but in these Bible verses it is explicitly spelled out. Aloes (commonly known as sandalwood today) and myrrh are, and were then, extremely precious spices. High quality oils are sold in very small containers today (typically 5-15 ml bottles). The spices brought for Jesus were undoubtedly highest quality. In today's market one hundred pounds of pure aloes and myrrh would sell for $150,000-$200,000. In some communities a home may be purchased for that sum. Some scholars believe a pound in the first century may have been a bit less than our pound today. The amount used may have been anywhere between seventy-five to a hundred pounds. The above value is based on one hundred pounds being purchased in small quantities of high quality oils.

[1] Rubin, Gail, CT, The Doyenne of Death®, "Jewish Burial Equals Green Burial," 2016, *A Good Goodbye, http://agoodgoodbye.com/news/articles/jewish-burial-equals-green-burial/*

A Woman of the Bible Displays the Fruit

Hannah Bites Her Tongue

Give people a piece of your heart, not a piece of your mind.[1]
~~Dr. Alan Zimmerman, CSP

We appropriately ooed and ahhed over the newborn visiting that day. Then the comments began. "When are you going to have one? You've been married long enough." Oh, the thoughtless words that spilled over from the non-stop chatter of a hair salon. There was no reply, just silence, as my daughter held back her tears.

Then the comments turned toward me. "You know you want to be a grandma. Go on. Tell her it's time." Difficulty conceiving had not been a challenge for me. Watching my child navigate this painful dilemma distressed me deeply. I hurt for my child and was helpless to change the circumstances.

An unsightly explosion brewed. Holding back the anger I felt, I'm certain my tongue bled 'til I could taste it. I shrugged my shoulders and may have commented, "This is not my choice to make." I knew how much she and her husband desired a child – we all did, but that wasn't happening. I'm very thankful the Holy Spirit's work in my heart allowed me to inhale the aroma of self-control and hold my tongue that day.

Scripture allows us a peak into Hannah's life. In a few short verses, we witness several gifts from the locked garden: love, peace, patience, faithfulness, and self-control. I'm convinced evidence of the others presented themselves on other days. She faithfully loved her husband, and he loved her in return. God loved her even more. Hannah prayed faithfully and patiently for many years for a child, while she maintained a peaceful relationship with Elkanah's other wife, Penninniah. God blessed Penniniah with several children, and she often taunted Hannah about her barrenness. Keeping peace with this woman required serious self-control. We're told Hannah cried and refused to eat, but lashing out at Peninniah is never mentioned. Self-control may be the last fruit in the Holy Spirit basket, and it may be the toughest one of all – tough for Hannah and tough for us.

Sandalwood comes from the heartwood of the tree. The tree must be destroyed to distill its oil.[2] The extent of reforestation necessary to meet the demand is high. To have self-control necessitates dying to self and living for Christ. Our sinful flesh creates a major pitfall here. Holding her tongue in response to the other wife, required self-control for Hannah. I needed it desperately in response to the insensitive questions posed. Either of us could have easily landed in the bottom of that ugly pit.

Hannah responded to her situation in prayer:
Crushed in soul, Hannah prayed to God and cried and cried—
inconsolably. Then she made a vow:
Oh, God-of-the-Angel-Armies
If you'll take a good, hard look at my pain,
If you'll quit neglecting me and go into action for me
By giving me a son,
I'll give him completely, unreservedly to you.
I'll set him apart for a life of holy discipline.
(1 Samuel 1:10-11, MSG)

God answered Hannah's prayers. He blessed Hannah and Elkanah with a son the next year. She kept the promise she made to God. After she weaned the child, she returned to the temple with him and dedicated him to the service of the Lord. She and Elkanah returned home where their family grew. They had sons and daughters, but Samuel remained special to mom. Every year they traveled to the temple to visit Samuel. Each time she brought a new cloak for her son. He was growing in his own relationship and love for God. (Read Hannah's story in 1 Samuel 1-2.)

In what situations are you most easily provoked? Are there strongholds in your heart needing to be crushed for you to gain control over your temper in moments when your pride and ego may be on the line? What importance do you place on the Holy Spirit's nurture of self-control in your heart no matter how difficult the pruning may be? Self-control is a sign of maturity. I first found Dr. Zimmerman's quote used by Victoria Green on her blog.[3] She stated it this way, and I love it: *"Maturing in Christ means giving someone a piece of your heart when you really want to give them a piece of your mind."* Now that's self-control!

Note: God could have chosen (for His glory) to have Hannah's story end much differently. Her womb could have remained closed. That could have happened to our daughter as well. Those outcomes would not have meant God loved either of them any less. Like Hannah's, eventually our family's prayers were also answered in the affirmative, and our daughter has two beautiful daughters of her own.

[1] Zimmerman, Dr. Alan, CSP, "Give People a Piece of Your Heart, Not a Piece of Your Mind," *Dr. Alan Zimmerman, CSP – The Positive Communication Pro, http://www.drzimmerman.com/tuesdaytip/we-need-relationships-to-survive*

[2] "Sandalwood Information," *Scents of the Earth, http://www.scents-of-earth.com/sandalwood1.html*

[3] Green, Victoria, *The Pretty Girl's Life, www.theprettygirlslife.com* This quote is no longer on the blog, but you may enjoy her reflections on living for Jesus as a lifestyle.

Aloes/Sandalwood – Essence Droplets

Charm is deceptive, and beauty is fleeting;
but a woman who fears the LORD is to be praised.
(Proverbs 31:30)

Fun facts about aloes

- Aloes are mentioned five times in Scripture. Four of those times it is linked with myrrh. [1] When diffused together their aromas enhance each other to create a delightful blend.
- Sandalwood blooms all year long.[2]
- Honeybees and ants are attracted to the flowers and keep the plants pollinated.[3]
- Each pea-sized round-shaped fruit of the sandalwood tree contains just one small seed.[4]
- The quality of the soil determines the intensity of the aroma of sandalwood. Trees that grow in the poorest soil often produce the higher quality essential oil.[5]
- A sandalwood tree is ready for harvest in thirty to sixty years. The tree gives up its life to produce the oil since it is made from the heartwood.[6]
- Each ton of heartwood produces approximately 90 pounds of essential oil. That's 4.5% yield per pound.[7]
- The sandalwood tree feeds on other plants around it.[8]
- In India sandalwood is carved into boxes, combs, beads, and statues like elephants. Many stores operate just to sell these sandalwood arts.[9]

Your turn

– Unfinished sandalwood beads are perfect for creating a bracelet diffuser. String on stretchy cord to desired length. Place a drop or two of any desired essential oil in the palm of your hand. Roll the beaded bracelet around in the oil. Wear and enjoy the scent all day. These are available ready-made on some of the hand-made crafts for sale sights online.

– Sleepy-Time Spray Mist

You'll need:

2 oz. Spray mist bottle

Witch hazel & distilled water

10 drops of lavender essential oil

5 drops of sandalwood essential oil

- Add the essential oils to the spray mist bottle.
- Fill the bottle with ½ witch hazel and ½ distilled water.
- Shake well.
- Mist your pillow at bedtime.

– Find a favorite recipe for homemade soap. Add sandalwood essential oil mixed with lemon, lavender, or frankincense essential oils for a pleasing start to your day.

Note: Sandalwood is one essential oil/plant material that figures prominently in pagan rituals. Remember God created all the plants. Sandalwood is mentioned (as aloes) five times in Scripture, and it was used by Nicodemus for Jesus' burial.

[1] *BibleGateway, https://www.biblegateway.com/quicksearch/?quicksearch=aloes&qs_version=HCSB*

[2] "Sandalwood Facts," *SoftSchools.com, http://www.softschools.com/facts/plants/sandalwood_facts/1977/*

[3] "Sandalwood Facts," *SoftSchools.com, http://www.softschools.com/facts/plants/sandalwood_facts/1977/*

[4] "Sandalwood Facts," *SoftSchools.com, http://www.softschools.com/facts/plants/sandalwood_facts/1977/*

[5] "Sandalwood Facts," *SoftSchools.com, http://www.softschools.com/facts/plants/sandalwood_facts/1977/*

[6] "Sandalwood Facts," *SoftSchools.com, http://www.softschools.com/facts/plants/sandalwood_facts/1977/*

[7] "Percent Yield Guide for Essential Oil Distillation," *The Essential Oil Company, https://www.essentialoil.com/pages/percentage-yield*

[8] "Santalum," *Wikipedia, https://en.wikipedia.org/wiki/Santalum*

[9] "Cultural & Historical," 2015, *Sandalwood Oil Specialist, http://sandalwoodoilspecialist.com/uses-of-sandalwood/cultural-historical/*

Chapter 10

Before You Go . . .

. . . A Few Parting Thoughts

You have ravished my heart, my sister, my bride, you have ravished my heart with a glance of your eyes, with one jewel of your necklace. How sweet is your love, my sister, my bride! How much better is your love than wine and the fragrance of your oils than any spice! Your lips distil nectar, my bride, honey and milk are under your tongue; the scent of your garments is like the scent of Lebanon.

(Song of Solomon 4:9-11, RSV)

In the Jewish tradition the bridegroom and his father prepare a home for the couple on land owned by the groom's father. The bride must remain prepared at all times, because she has no idea when the groom will come for her.

Every book of the Bible bears testimony to Jesus Christ. Never once mentioned by name in the Song of Solomon, the reference is implied. Son of King David, Solomon represents Christ. Jesus descended from the line of David. The bride portrays the beauty of the Bride of Christ – the church – all who believe in Him and who follow Him. The essence of the oils, spices, and nectars reveals the work of the Holy Spirit in the bride's life.

So, why is her garden locked? For certain she has kept herself pure for her groom. Making preparations in the secret place, her beauty went temporarily unnoticed by detractors. Seclusion protected her from temptations that soiled her wedding attire.

She found ample time to meditate and allow her garden to be tended. Opportunities abounded to see God up close and personal.

Her inner appearance transformed at the same time outward preparations and bridal fittings enhanced her physical beauty. She stood ready for her groom's unannounced arrival.

She held the key to the gate, coming and going as she needed. She locked out those who would steal her purity, giving intimacy only to her true love. Because she prepared in secret, his surprises were many.

Father and son together prepared a home for the betrothed couple. Coming unannounced, the bridegroom escorted her and their guests to the wedding feast. Their procession radiated beauty. Wisdom flowed from her secret fountain brimming with Living Water. Billowing essences of fruit from her well-tended garden could not be held back. Her groom and their guests were blessed. To God be the glory.

Awaken, north wind—
come, south wind.
Blow on my garden,
and spread the fragrance of its spices.
Let my love come to his garden
and eat its choicest fruits.
(Song of Solomon 4:16, RSV)

When Jesus makes His unannounced return for His Bride He leads the procession in radiance beyond measure to His Father's home. Together He and the Father prepared The Wedding Feast of the Lamb in the New Jerusalem. There are gates there too, but they will always be open, because there is no more night. We will live in the streams of the Living Water, Jesus Christ Himself.

In the daytime (for there will be no night there) its gates will never be closed; and they will bring the glory and the honor of the nations into it; and nothing unclean, and no one who practices abomination and lying, shall ever come into it, but only those whose names are written in the Lamb's book of life.

(Revelation 21:25, NASB)

Note: Both King David's death and Solomon's engagement and marriage to the Shulamite woman took place the same year.[1] We have no way to know if father and son finished the couple's new home together, or if King David was in attendance at the wedding. We can be absolutely sure from Scripture that Jesus and our Heavenly Father will be present at the Marriage Supper of the Lamb, and those who believe and follow Jesus will live with them forever!

If you loved this inspirational collection, please leave a review on Amazon.com

We love to hear from you, our readers:

- Sign up for our email list at www.LynnUWatson.com – we will send you a FREE GIFT when you do.
- Visit our blog www.LynnUWatson.com/blog. We welcome your comments.
- Follow us on Facebook (leave comments and share, too, please) www.facebook.com/lynnuwatsonwriter
- And we are on Pinterest. www.pinterest.com/lynnuwatson
- Recipes featured at Cinnmah-Brosia's Coffee Cottage and gifts available in her gift shop are found on the website: www.LynnUWatson.com
- In need of a website of your own. Thank you for considering www.watsondesign.us

[1] Dates found on timelines from: *The Study Bible for Women*, Copyright © 2014 by Holman Bible Publishers, Nashville, Tennessee. All Rights Reserved., pages 406, 845.

Cinnamah-Brosia's Profile

Birth Name: Cinnamon Amber Porter

Current Name: Cinnamon Amber (Porter) Fields

Nickname: Cinnamah-Brosia

Aliases: C-B, Cinnabro, Ms Cimmaba, Cinna-B, and many others her friends create

Birthday: May 14, 1970

Place of Birth: Pearlville, Missouri

Gender: Female

Eye Color: Green

Hair Color: Dark brown with rich red highlights
Height: 5'5"

Mother: Sandra Marie (Madison) Porter   1953

Father: Andrew (Andy) Robert Porter   1951

Siblings: Blossom Heather (Porter) Griffin   1971
         Stone Andrew Porter   1975

Maternal Grandmother: Dorothy Elizabeth (Perkins) Madison – a.k.a. Miss Dot)   1929-2016

Maternal Grandfather: Benjamin Henry Madison (Ben)   1926-2001

Education: Registered Nurse; completed nursing school May 1990

Husband: Jeremy Thomas Fields June 12, 1967

Wedding Date: May 12, 1990

Children: Kaitlyn Dorothy Fields, born November 10, 1994

Aaron Thomas Fields, born May 22, 1995

Caryn Joy Fields, bornNovember 24, 1999

Transportation: "Ruby," her bright red cruiser bicycle

Hobbies: aromatherapy, gardening, biking, all kinds of crafts (she rarely finds time for), reading, baking, entertaining, making others smile, she's dreaming of others she hasn't shared yet

Miss Dot's Café opened in 1966. After her passing in early 2016, Miss Dot's will provided funding specifically to renovate the cottage. Her grandmother and Kaitlyn envisioned the changes, and Cinnamah-Brosia promised Gram they would happen. The café would maintain its neighborly role in the community. A women's small group, formed several years earlier, continued to meet at the cottage during the construction phase. Although sometimes a challenge, they loved every minute of being part of, what they considered, community history in the making. In October 2016, Miss Dot's Café officially reopened as Cinnamah-Brosia's Coffee Cottage and Gift Shop.

Sophia's Corner: A stone fireplace as the backdrop, the corner is furnished with a gingerbread leather sofa and other comfy seating. The women's group meets here. It's rearranged a bit to be the "stage" area for musicians on Saturday nights when it opens as Fish and Beans Coffee House at the cottage. Sophia means wisdom in Greek, but it became known by that name in honor of the calico cat hanging around Miss Dot's Café. Gram called her Sophia, because she was wise enough to know where she would be loved and fed.

Fish and Beans Coffee House: In the early 1970's, Gram and Gramps opened Miss Dot's Café on Saturday evenings as a coffee house hangout for teens. Local musicians led those who attended in Jesus movement songs popular at the time. Coffee, of course, is made from beans, and fish made the name because of its symbolic connection to Christianity. Cinnamah-Brosia and friends revived the tradition at the coffee cottage.

Sign displayed above the coffee cottage's menu board:
> Let all those you encounter leave happier
> and better than they were before:
> Have gentleness in your eyes – loving-kindness in your smile.
> ~~Unknown

Cinnamah-Brosia's friends – in the order you meet them:

Jane – long-time friend – helped in the café and helps in the coffee cottage, too – leads the women's group that meets there

Frank – editor of the local Pearlville Weekly

Lily – six-year-old daughter of Mandy & Chase

Mandy – Lily's mom – married to Chase – local church connection with missionary family

Vanessa – child of the missionary family

Sara – regular, but rather unknown guest at Cinnamah-Brosia's Coffee Cottage and Gift Shop

Carol – lost a baby and remembers Miss Dot's kindness to her

Melanie – Troubled in her teens, remembers Miss Dot's encouragement

Pastor Rick – pastored the church Cinnamah-Brosia and Jeremy attended early in their marriage

Jennifer – she and husband, Craig, learned a big lesson when purchasing a new home

Susan – she and husband, Mark, received a most unexpected answer to a long time prayer request

Melissa – bookstore owner, next-door neighbor to Mark's parents

Haley – married to Dan – couple has a whole string of setbacks that have Haley questioning God

Crystal – married to Jeff – she's been coming to the café since she was a little girl (with her mom); has a little girl (Josie)

Holt – one of the musicians who plays on Fish and Beans night

Star – she and Cinnamah-Brosia lead a Bible study for at-risk teen girls

Pastor Gary – pastor of local church – officiated at Cinnamah-Brosia and Jeremy's wedding

Allie – Caryn's best friend

Miss Alice – Carol's mom – one of Gram's best friends – she and husband, George, have retired and moved away

You are personally invited to join Cinnamah-Brosia and her friends throughout the year by visiting our blog: www.LynnUWatson.com/blog

Lynn posts regular updates, and you'll find a menu board there too, with links to the recipes featured at the coffee cottage.

Coming in 2017 – in time for the holidays:

Cinnamah-Brosia's Coffee Cottage

Inspirational Collection for Women – Volume 2:

The Essence of Joy

Resources

Father Juan Arintero, G. O. P., *The Song of Songs,* (Cincinnati, Ohio: The English edition first published by The Dominican Nuns, formerly of the Monastery of the Holy Name, 1974. Rockford, Illinois: Tan Books and Publishers, Inc., 1992).

Connie and Alan Higley, *Reference Guide for Essential Oils,* (Spanish Fork, Utah: Abundant Health, 1996-2012, Thirteenth Edition revised January 2012).

Hannah Hurnard, *Mountain of Spices*, (American edition, Wheaton, Illinois: Tyndale House, 1977).

Vincenzina Krymow, *Healing Plants of the Bible: History, Lord & Meditations,* (Cincinnati, Ohio: St. Anthony Messenger Press, 2002).

John Lawton, *Silk Scents & Spice*, (Paris, France: UNESCO Publishing, 2004).
Herbert Lockyer, All the Women of the Bible, (Grand Rapids, Michigan: Zondervan, 1967).

Lytton John Musselman, *Figs, Dates, Laurel, and Myrrh: Plants of the Bible and the Quran,* (Portland, Oregon: Timber Press, 2007).

Ann Spangler, and Jean E. Syswerda, *Women of the Bible*, (Grand Rapids, Michigan: Zondervan, 1999.

David Stewart, Ph.D., *Healing Oils of the Bible,* (Mable Hill, Missouri: Care Publications, 2003).

Allan A. Swenson, *Plants of the Bible and How to Grow Them*, (New York, New York: Kensington Publishing Corp., 1995).

D. Gary Young, *The One Gift*, (Orem Utah: YL Wisdom, 2010).

OTHER:

Many websites were used to gather the information in this inspirational collection. They are included as footnotes in each chapter. All links were active at the time of publication. If link is no longer available please use your search engine to find the info on another website.

Lynn uses the Young Living™ brand of essential oils. There are other quality brands of essential oils on the market. We recommend you research the options and choose high quality oils within your budget.

Disclaimers

Cinnamah-Brosia is a fictional character. All similarities to real life people you know are totally intentional, but she is a little bit of all of us. Real women's stories were used and fictionalized (with permission) to flow with her character and the setting. We hope you found yourself and your friends right there on the coffee cottage pages. It's a great place to hang out.

Content of this book:

None of the statements in this book have been evaluated by the FDA. The information contained in this book and in any references cited is for educational and inspirational purposes only. It is not provided to diagnose, prescribe, or treat or cure any health condition. The information should not be used as a substitute for medical counseling. Caution should be exercised when using essential oils. You are responsible for educating yourself and consulting with health care professionals in any and all matters regarding the use of essential oil or other plant-based products. The author accepts no responsibility for such use. Please consult with your health care professional for all your health care needs.

Some essential oils are unsafe or should be used with great caution for children and pregnant women. Consult your medical professional before use, and educate yourself about uses and cautions.

Young Living Essential Oils™ has not endorsed any part of this book. The author is not receiving any compensation associated with this book from Young Living Essential Oils™ or any other essential oil company. No essential oil company, including but not limited to Young Living Essential Oils™, is responsible for the information in this book.

Acknowledgements

A few notes of thanks are absolutely necessary. An amazing group of friends and family have contributed so much for you to be holding The Essence of Courage in your hands. I pray no one has been overlooked.

My husband, Steve – You endure my many crazy projects and still love me. The website and other graphics are amazing because of your talents!

Lynda – You introduced me to essential oils, and look how far the journey has come.

Johnnie – Your invitation to the Mid-South Christian Writer's Conference opened doors to what for 12 years had only been a dream.

Robin – You've walked with me through many wild adventures. I'm so grateful you were with me all the way through this one, too. And your insights added so much.

Allisha – Cinnamah-Brosia pops off the page and welcomes us all in to the coffee cottage because of your artistic gift. Thank you for envisioning her and creating her image.

Helen – You caught the vision with me. What a God story from the night we first met. Thanking Him for our friendship and the opportunity to work together to bring this devotional to life.

Amy, Bonnie, Carolyn, Gayelynn, Joyce, Londa, Margaret, Sandra, and Tina – Sharing your stories, they became Cinnamah-Brosia's stories. You made her the lovable friend she is, looking a bit like each of us.

My family – My stories are our stories. I love you more than you will ever know and love doing life with you.

Elizabeth – We became friends, because I attended the Mid-South Christian Writer's Conference. This book is so much better because of your editing magic.

Sole Hope – You allowed Cinnamah-Brosia to host a shoe cutting party at Fish and Beans without knowing much about this project at all. Thank you for your trust.

Carrie, Erin, Jagoda, Jeanne, Jennifer, Joyce, Karen, Noelle, Sammy, Sharron – You accepted the responsibility of being the first readers of this devotional. Your thoughts, encouragement, and friendship (new or old) mean the world.

Our Faithful God –
He provides my essence of courage every single day.

Dear New Friend,

There is an old campfire song that speaks of the treasure of friendship: "Make new friends, but keep the old. One is silver and the other gold."

Thank you for stopping by and hanging with my friends and me. We've thoroughly enjoyed your company, and already feel like you've become our new best and treasured friend.

Friendship involves sharing. You've heard our stories. We would love to hear yours, too. We all learn so much from each other, and relationships grow.

Our next volume in this collection, *The Essence of Joy,* provides opportunities for us to creatively share your stories. Join Lynn's email list.* As calls for stories are posted, you'll be among the first to know.

Please stop by often. We'll do friends, coffee, and Jesus! Looking forward to our adventures.

Hugs,
Cinnamah-Brosia

*Sign-up form for our email list is found on the homepage at www. LynnUWatson.com